The Windows *of* Reality

Ibogaine for Opiate Addiction
-One Man's Ibogaine Experience-

Written by Drug War Veteran and Two-time National Science Foundation Award Winning Author:

Timothy Allen Zigler

TRUTH FLASHER BOOKS

23573 South Malnetta Road Crown King, Arizona 86343

This book is a work of non-fiction. Most of the names and some of the places have been changed to protect the privacy of those who do not wish to make public their situations. Most of the story's setting locations in Mexico *and* the United States have not been changed. Other than the Author and the public figures mentioned, resemblance of the main story's characters to actual persons is merely coincidental. Besides the variations listed herein, everything in this book is 100% true according to the Author's perception of his personal experience.

Dedication – "Story Time"

It is to the other half of my undying heart that I dedicate this "Story-Time." When my wife Katie and I began dating, after a night of partying we would have "Story-Time" until we would both fall asleep. For years after we had begun dating, Katie had no idea where I even came from. So, "Story-Time" was shocking. "Story-Time" is the ritual to which I owe this book. I had built my walls of disguise so high that I had even forgotten where I had come from.

Katie and I might have been tipsy from a holiday party or on a vacation night and the "stories" got crazier and crazier. Katie encouraged me to be whomever I chose to be at the moment.

Thank you, Katie, for allowing me to spend 20 hours a day many times – and for allowing me to spend a stupid amount of money making this book – "if only for the chance of helping one other soul." Katie, you always encouraged me to make "Story-Time" a jacket, so here you go.

There are no "writers" in this world, only people who are lucky enough to have both a lot of time on their hands, and good enough things to write about. Thanks for making me a writer, Katie. I look forward to paying you back for the rest of my life. You can now have, "Story Time," whenever you like.

Thank You, Katie, for knowing I was worth saving!

Table of Contents

1.

In-Doctor-Nation

My older brother, Joey, was my hero, but he wasn't as lucky as my younger brother, Nathan, and I were. Joey, died of a heroin overdose in his early 30s, and left behind three young children, two of whom probably do not remember him. Joey had started on *Ritalin* before he was a teenager. That quickly inflated into a massive fishing-tackle box, containing a pharmacopia of pills, which he never left home without.

The tackle-box which Joey had satirically dubbed, "The Presidential Football," was next to him when Joey laid cold with crusty foam trailing from his mouth. His body was contorted in a boxer pose, and when my dad saw him, he said his Joey's skin had so discolored that Joey had reminded him of *The Incredible Hulk*. I hate to admit this, but, I also was a cover-up artist for the *Evil Empire* at the time, so I told everyone that Joey had died of a heart attack. Today I am finally ready to face the truth of these matters with you.

My younger brother was injured in a steel mill accident decades prior and had miraculously saved himself from a substantial amount of prescribed methadone, also taken for a decade. Nathan never could shake the *Xanax*, a benzodiazepine. That is a hard task to accomplish. There are other abuses currently going on in the family, but, it's still *going on* so you get the picture.

My good friend, and nearly family member—my sister-in-law's brother—had died in a car accident. My wife, Katie, and I were at "Dax's" funeral when I got the news about Joey's death. As we drove out of the graveyard through those black, wrought iron cemetery gates, I listened to my voicemail. Dad had for some reason left a message to give me the news:

"Tim, it's Dad. They just found Joey dead at your little brother's house."
—Allen Zigler—

I'm sorry, since I'm sure you've probably lost or are losing someone right now, and no one wants to see this. But I thought my brother Joey's killers ought to have to share that disgusting moment with us.

At the mature age of 39, I was an ordinary person just like yourself. I lived in Scottsdale, Arizona, in the foothills of Thompson Peak, right behind West World; That's where they hold the Barrett-Jackson Auto Auction. The Phoenix Open is also held right around the corner; it's a gorgeous part of the globe.

I had a business, 2.0 kids, a career, a dog named Lollipop, a church, and well, unfortunately, I had also had a brutal, prescription-pill slash heroin problem for ten years straight. It didn't start with the heroin, but I'll get back to that.

Being well beyond the honeymoon stage in my relationship with painkillers, I was now on a great quest to cure my *incurable disease.* After being betrayed by the same medical providers who had assigned me the label, I had tried everything. The only known remedy to my incurable disease was more doctor prescribed pills, a methodology for treatment to which I no longer subscribed.

I was pretty good at acting human, but I wasn't a human anymore; what did remain was a shadow of my former self. I tried imagining what it had felt like being opiate naive but had no recollection from then. Every morning I woke up sick until I had had my morning fix. Afterward, I again felt nothing. Every evening ended with chemically putting myself to sleep using the same mechanism with which I had started my day. There were times when I felt euphoria or extra energy, but those times faded after becoming physically dependent, and that is where the lie ended.

A great, one man worldwide quest then began for a magic bullet for which I was willing to pay any price, monetary or otherwise. But, if I didn't find that magic bullet soon, I was going to use a full-metal-jacket, which is painless and would have only cost my heirs twenty-five cents. A dear friend lived in the same dark place as I; he shared my passion for the great quest. *'Jack'* wasn't as eager as I was to risk his ordinary reputation. Many times we discussed the wacky detox methods we had come across in our research. Plenty of "cures" circulated amongst fellow junkies, the media, and the misinformation mills referred to as websites.

One of the more demented detox methods I'd seen, came from a heroin user whom I'd met through Jack. I had exhausted my prescription early, and was buying even more pills from the junkie; the drug-dealer was "kicking" heroin, and so immediately had my attention. His rehabilitation protocol? He'd been mainlining crystal methamphetamine and had been "clean for four days."

The junkie administered the intravenous treatment to mute the physical withdrawal symptoms.

The junkie held an ounce of black-tar heroin in his hands at all times, as an additional measure for dealing with the mental separation from his vile brown-mistress. "I'll prove I have the willpower to beat this thing," the junkie boasted. He was out of his tree, chewing invisible bubblegum, and licked his lips excessively. His head made sudden movements for viewing objects that didn't appear to exist. A glance to his lap produced the image of two filthy-hands, squeezing and kneading a brown ball with which he had stained them.

The junkie lost me at meth therapy, but his story is one example of the extremes people will go to escape that drug's tight grip. Here's a shocker: it didn't work. After relapsing, he later won his opiate battle in prison where he involuntarily detoxed in a cell, that is until he was released. The junkie was one of many sketchy characters with whom I had now found myself fraternizing after work when I should have been safely at home with the family.

On yet another pill buying excursion, I met Jack in a dark drugstore parking lot. We sat visiting in his pick-up after the transaction. Jack had heard about *Iboga* through his lady-friend, who was a 20-year heroin addict; she wanted to undergo *Ibogaine treatment* when her
"settlement came in." After hearing about so many extraordinary remedies over the years, I didn't have my hopes up.

"It's a psychedelic drug," Jack said.

"Like *LSD*?"

"No, I think it's LSD's big evil brother; a harrowing seventy-two-hour psychedelic experience is a side-effect of the medicine. The drug is illegal in America so you'd have to leave the country. Oh, and it's expensive as hell."

"Let me see if I have this right. Ibogaine treatment works like this: junkie goes to see the witchdoctor. Junkie takes the hokey African-root-bark remedy. Junkie trips balls for three days, in the hands of complete strangers, in a third world country. Only after junkie pays spiritual-piper, is he delivered from opiate addiction?"

"Yeah. That's a sarcastic way of putting it, Tim, but, YES, they claim exactly that. The clinicians claim you can binge right up until the day-of. One day you're a junkie, the next – POOF – you wake up a real human again. The internet shows it can cure addicts of any addiction; Ibogaine even heals emotional trauma caused by child abuse, PTSD, or any other emotional baggage, also – POOF – goes away. There's never a need for an additional pill."

"No way. If that were true, there wouldn't be a single drug-addict in the US. Our government wouldn't allow that, would they? Okay, when you call, does a man named Jim, with a thick Nigerian accent pick-up the telephone and ask you to wire him a deposit with a prepaid *Green Dot card?"* I kidded.

"No dude, I think it's legit. This is the one," the friend assured.

After filing the Ibogaine remedy right next to the junkie's meth solution, I continued home. Upon arrival at my ordinary Scottsdale, Arizona, home, I headed straight for my laptop. I just couldn't get that Ibogaine remedy thing out of my head. Research began. I discovered plenty of amazing testimonials, but there was a vast quantity of mortifying data as well. For example, the 1/300 death rate. I again shelved the idea.

My wife, Katie, was my biggest fan. That woman had been through more than any person ought to have to endure (not all of which I had put her through, but we'll get back to that soon). We were good middle-class citizens with two beautiful girls, ages 21 and 12.

Our older daughter had skipped the third grade when we moved her from a good Catholic school to a better Christian school. She chose the medical profession, was on track to graduate nursing school within months, and was set to do so at the top of her class. Our younger daughter is as smart. She's a hell of a club volleyball player, a straight-A student who is in the National Junior Honor Society (NJHS), and we can't tell the two apart on the phone.

Katie tolerated my problem but clearly didn't like it. She continuously found creative ways to express her disapproval of my personal catastrophe. Having ridden shotgun for the entire trip, Katie understood the complexities of my dilemma as much as anyone who has never been in my position could.

She watched me detox cold turkey six years ago. For 17 hellish days, I barely sleep a second. I collapsed from exhaustion, waking up in a puddle of sweat after sleeping only 22 minutes. I finally relapsed four months of agony later; it never got better. I had begun to believe reality just sucked, and I had only forgotten how bad it was.

So herein was the problem: Where does one find several months of spare time for such an appointment with satan? Could it take even longer than six months? What about after that? Would I ever truly be happy again? Regardless of the "complexities," pressure mounted as the appointment with satan grew closer-and-closer.

I told Katie, "I'll handle it after Thanksgiving." When Thanksgiving rolled around, I granted myself an extension through Christmas and New Year's. I didn't want to "ruin the holidays." Always in the throes of writing proposals, there was never a right time, but the real truth is, I didn't see a way out, and that scared me.

Existential anxiety began devouring my late nights. I'd never been afraid of dying. Thinking back, I might have been afraid of myself? Finally, I became fed up with myself and my addiction. No longer could I lie about where I'd been and how much I had used. A tornado of suicidal hate, guilt, financial expense, and pressure from Katie swallowed me whole. Oh, and, at the time, I was urinating pure blood as well. If I had a "rock bottom," that was it.

I decided to pay the Ibogaine thing another visit since I was out of reasonable options. Arguments from both sides of the debate made sense. The truth is that my mind was made-up, even before I began my research. The research was only a way of selecting information to build a case for Katie, who is a color-inside-the-lines sort.

It may seem reckless to you, but I was going to do it. There were two statistics in particular which had piqued my interest in Ibogaine.

First – the supposed recovery time. Most of the information I found on the internet, implied that the treatment would take from one to two weeks. That was perfect; I'd be back at work before I knew it.

Second – the '1/300 death rate.' Sadly, this time, the 1/300 mortality rate had interested me the most. If the treatment were a hoax, I hoped to die there, wherever *there* would be.

"Wherever *there* would be" was my next question. So, I turned my attention to facilities around the world. The first place I contacted was in Costa Rica and employed a *Bwiti Shaman* for delivering the psychedelic. The Shaman stuffed his victims full of African root-bark until they purged. Um… During that method, the Shaman kept you on your feet for up to 72 hours of introspective hallucination. NOT FOR ME!

On *Joe Rogan Experience*, podcast #195, Mixed Martial Arts (MMA) fighter, Aubrey Marcus, mentioned the potential anti-addictive properties of Ibogaine, though, Marcus himself was not an addict. The warrior bravely shared a story of one such heroin addict who shared the hut with him and his girlfriend in Costa Rica. The Shaman explained: "I will feed him so much Iboga, he will never want to touch heroin again."

Turning my attention toward other facilities, those with a more clinical focus. I now looked at Canada, Panama, Peru, and Mexico – all countries where the treatment is legal. I chose Mexico, only for its proximity to Arizona. I know, I know: Great! I'd been Google-imaging something only weeks ago and a picture of ten severed human heads presented itself during the search.

Someone had posed the silent and truncated crowd on a street corner in Acapulco, behind a cardboard sign which had donned some Sharpie-scrawled cartel propaganda. I turned the computer toward Katie and shouted, "HEY LOOK!" That didn't improve my case for *the treatment* with Katie.

I phoned a doctor associated with a facility in "beautiful Rosarito, Mexico." The clinic was in the country's northwestern-most-state of Baja-California, only miles south of San Diego. Doctor Pollardo spoke with a matter-of-fact tone, and his treatment center sounded like traditional drug rehab.

Negotiation of his sale price ensued since I never expected to find a fun place to detox anyhow, but, at least, Pollardo's place seemed somewhat safe. I offered $7,000 for the $10,000 treatment. The doctor agreed to my price after my commitment to join his "last minute waiting list." From Dr. Pollardo's tone, in combination with the nature of his craft, I gathered that "backing out," was commonplace. We closed the deal, but I was still somewhat uneasy about the place. I don't know... Something didn't feel right.

I called one last place, only to see who would answer the phone. It was a joint by the name of "Ibogaine University," and an American by the name of John Charleston picked-up. YAHTZEE! An American guy with an American accent – SOLD! No medical questions, no nothing. John's personal story didn't hurt either.

"I was a biochemistry student, and while attending a prestigious SoCal college, I got hooked on heroin while experimenting with drugs of all sorts. At the beginning of my final semester, I cashed in my single remaining chance for recovery. Using the balance of my college fund, I went to Mexico for Ibogaine treatment. I sold everything for that miracle, and I'm thankful I did too; the treatment saved my life."

John had now made his home in Mexico to save others, as a result of being moved by the experience. Well, well, well, guess who urgently yearned for salvation? This guy. I informed John of his esteemed colleague's willingness to treat for the low, low price of seven thousand dollars, to which John replied: "Okay, but that's it."

I had already bought the treatment, and now my oral presentation was finally ready for Katie. My impromptu performance came one arid Arizona-winter night, in 2014 while Katie speed-watched her typical daily regimen of recorded "Reality TV." Following a brief opening statement, during which I ignored the 1/300 mortality rate and the Mexico locale, I convincingly opened my laptop.

Exhibit A – Show Katie testimonials from people who have attempted the crazy ritual before. Katie paused her TV and viewed my laptop screen for several minutes. I felt her super-focus, as western medicine's worst nightmare unfolded on my laptop screen.

I thought to myself: I'm pretty sure this is working, at which point she loudly asked, "What are you thinking? Both of my parents are millionaires, love you to death, and would do anything for you, so why would you even consider that? No! You are NOT going to Mexico for any such medical treatment."

Katie and I both knew the potential consequences of my problem. My brother's untimely death was always a lingering reminder of that, and it is also what gave me the okay to *compulsively* consume painkillers.

Changing her tactics, Katie asked, "What about drug rehab?"

A couple, friends of Katie's father and with whom we often golfed on Sundays, had lost a son to a painkiller OD several years prior. Austin died within weeks of my oldest brother's heroin overdose. Austin's parents began a foundation to collect donations for their cause. There has been an annual fundraiser golf tournament every year following. All funds raised are used for rehabilitation of us sick and tormented souls.

I won the charter tournament's putting contest and re-donated the winnings to the cause. I wouldn't have felt right leaving a fundraiser with more cash than I'd come in with. Katie's dad was a principal donor from day one of the charter.

Katie asked, "Why don't I call and see if Austin's mom will reserve a bed for you?"

Within a year or so of those two overdose deaths, I'd lost all three remaining grandparents. I think the subsequent loss gave me the permission needed for using sub-toxic levels of the medicine with no regard for my personal safety. All of those tragic events seemed to dampen my argument with Katie, more than a little.

A good friend, who lived in our neighborhood, happened to be CEO of one of the largest nonprofit chains of drug and alcohol rehabilitation centers in the world. Quite often I'd give her grief, kiddingly of course, that she was the "CEO of the world's largest bed and breakfast." Many times we would have drinks with the couple on a Friday or Saturday night. Her husband was a funny son-of-a-bitch.

The first time we ever went out with them, I remember, for no apparent reason, he intermittently stood up and introduced members of our party. He did so as if he were *Ed McMahon* by randomly and arbitrarily announcing individuals who'd been sitting there for hours. Out of nowhere, he would announce, "Katie Zigler, Ladies and Gentlemen!" An announcement began with his clapping and continued with one or two others, who would awkwardly join in. The outbursts ended in simultaneous bouts of laughter and applause from the entire group, every time he repeated the silly behavior; it never got old.

"Drug rehab is a miserable opiate detox. It requires a 30-90 day inpatient commitment. And, for the most part, it doesn't work," I argued with Katie. "I don't wanna be perceived as the family drug addict. For this method of treatment, the internet indicates, I'll be back to work in as little as a week," I snapped.

Katie's father was from the old-school, and once you were labeled something like a "drug addict," that's just what you were; Katie's "color-in-the-lines" mentality was surely a genetic gift from her "old man." During the holidays, if I were to look at an alcoholic beverage for too long, after that sort of public announcement, I'd have been given the hairy-eyeball. I didn't want that sort of stigma. Things didn't quite go as planned, but at least, I had sown the small seed.

2.

The American Nightmare

Months passed during which time I carefully rebuilt my case for Katie. Again I approached her and this time seemed different. I think she wanted it so badly for us that she would have forced herself to buy what I was selling.

I had become more isolated and withdrawn as my addiction escalated; it happened so fast. I was no longer in attendance at our social gatherings. I only left home to work my two jobs, which were a demanding seven-day a week operation. The only other reason I'd get-out - you guessed it, for scoring dope when my copious prescription ran out.

I remember the final time asking my doctor to increase the dosages, so I could once again legally stretch my script to my next appointment. (It had worked dozens of times before.) For the first time, he looked at me and said, "Tim, the amount of oxycodone you're using is triple what I prescribe for most of my terminal cancer patients; I simply can't." Terminal cancer patients? The feeling of dread poured over my being. My problem had reached terminal velocity, and Katie was finally ready for my presentation.

As ready, at least, as she'd ever be. *This time, I had polished up my sales pitch a little bit.*

The new sales pitch included a call to Mexico during which I placed John on speaker so Katie might share the same "Yahtzee" moment I had experienced. It worked and, while reluctant, she agreed to give it a chance.

It's funny how a familiar element sometimes lends a false sense of comfort to a dangerous situation. Katie had no choice in the matter since I had made it clear that I would be going, regardless.

During the phone call, I could tell that Katie was frightened at what we'd both "agreed upon" for the first time. That moment felt like we'd both decided to pull the plug on a couple of old friends in hospice. For the first time, we both had agreed to surrender. I resigned to the prospect of living a clean life which would allow me to rejoin the "real world." And Katie abandoned her insecurities and fears, which happened to be well-founded in that case.

Katie didn't even like staying home alone when I was out of town on business. Her acceptance of *the treatment* had now strangely provided robust conditions for my previously ignored fears to thrive in. Out of fear alone, I began to revisit the website on which the clinic John represented sold their program online.

Upon closer inspection, I was shocked to see that there were many typos within its text. It had appeared that Ibogaine University had hastily thrown together its website, which was quite disturbing. I kept the inconsistencies to myself since I knew they'd be great cause for concern for Katie. Continued phone calls to Ibogaine University produced strings of F-bombs from John's tongue. These bombarded my ears as he became more and more familiar with me.

Since 9/11, the American border had tightened its security and policies to meet the escalated threat of 'terrorism.' United States citizens were now required to have passports when visiting Mexico. I brought that up to John to which he proudly proclaimed, "I've gotten Americans through the Mexican border with no ID at all."

I'd been extremely skilled at hiding things in life that didn't seem to add-up, that worried me, or that affected me in a negative way. These skills came in particularly handy during my shitty childhood. Against my better judgment, I rejected every shred of what I read, saw, and heard about John and Ibogaine University. The many inconsistencies were filed right alongside all manner of other prior negativity and wrong-ness.

I'm not your typical drug addict; I have two great jobs, and I am mildly successful at both of them. A few years ago, I wrote my first winning National Science Foundation Small Business Innovation Research proposal. The Award came with a large sum of money, which I then budgeted for research and development of the technology I'd invented. The business had been in the local paper in my mother's hometown and state. We only waited for the finished prototype for the finalization of our national and international press releases.

I formed the business around the technology and located the brick and mortar in my mother's hometown of over thirty years. My company was established there out of convenience for my business partner who was disabled. I telecommuted that job Monday through Thursday, but it required me to make one or two trips back home per month, as well.

When traveling to Arkansas for business, I always stayed at my mother's place; she spoiled me with the most fantastic cooking. Mom had better financial and social stability than she had possessed during my childhood. Her prior absence had seemingly caused her to overcompensate with unnecessary cooking volume and excessive accommodation. I loved it but didn't take advantage as one of my siblings did.

On one such Arkansas business trip, a funny thing happened: My stepfather and I went to the hardware store together to purchase a tool. (I'm fairly handy, so I usually received a little punch-list from mom when getting home.) When we arrived at the check-out lane and the clerk noticed who I was, I had no idea who he was.

"Tim," he said.

"Yessir," I replied. I *do* bring back a taste of the local vernacular upon my arrival. (While engaged in that particular dialect of the English-language, one experiences a real sense of sincerity and friendship. It is a beautiful tongue for expression.)

"Do you mind if I walk around this here counter to shake your hand?" the man asked.

(My next-door-neighbors in Scottsdale won't even wave back at me when I make that mistake. Was I caught in the crossfire of some theatrical-arts flash-mob fusion?)

I looked back at my step-dad, who now wore his smile so big that his dark mustache stretched from ear-to-ear. He held his ball cap in his hands at waist level to gesture respect for the old man. Stepdad's hair was untidy, due to his excessive hat wearing problem; the hat suited him. Bunches of black curls flipped-up from the headband of his ball cap—he was getting gray. Looking again at my stepfather, I pointed at my chest inquisitively; I thought the clerk was joshing.

"Yeah, you. I wanna shake the hand of the man who's doin' all those wonderful thangs."

At first I thought it to be a joke, but it wasn't. The man walked around the counter and issued me the most sincere handshake I'd ever received. He was a true Southern gentleman. I was flattered, but the formality of it all was a bit uncomfortable.

That was a welcomed moment in comparison with my checkered past. On more than one occasion, my mom came home from the grocery store completely disappointed in me. That was where my parent-teacher conferences would usually go down. Twice my English teacher told my mother in the *Kroger's* check-out-lane that I'd be the perfect candidate for prison; it's hard to get away with anything in a small town.

No one in Mom's small town was wise to my problem. That is until I ran out of legal dope while back for a meeting. Here is how evil opiates are. As mad as I was at the doctor who killed Joey, I went and saw him for a Band-Aid prescription for preventing sickness until I got home. (It was the same doctor who had given Joey that tackle-box full of drugs since he was young.)

Even that son-of-a-bitch couldn't believe how much dope my doctor was giving me. He wouldn't even prescribe me what I was taking, much less, the volume.

I think he gave me 30x10mg Percocet (that's 30 tabs of 10 mg each of the Percocet) until I flew back to Scottsdale. I ran out before the end of the first day and never stopped sweating, sneezing, and borderline shitting myself; I was so sick. Walking into that doctor's office was one of the hardest and most disgusting things I have ever done.

It was not long after Joey's killer had been released from prison for a multimillion-dollar, Medicaid wheelchair scam. Apparently being a doctor isn't much like other jobs. Neither of my jobs would have allowed me to defraud the government, go to prison and just walk back out and start doing my job again. (And, in Joey's doctor's case, his job was killing people like my brothers and me for money.)

For my second job, I worked on the weekends from Friday through Sunday. I was a *'deal closer'* at the family car dealership.

My father-in-law was a principal partner and General Manager of "the store," which was one of the largest Japanese car stores in the world. I had worked at the dealership off-and-on over the prior twenty years. My father-in-law was among the coolest people I knew. There weren't a lot of guys whom you could say that about, but, thankfully, *I could.* He was also a dear friend to me, calling me "The Vice-President," at the family functions.

Between my closing car deals, we sat in his large posh office, which he'd had most conspicuously designed, just off the center of the showroom floor. The shelves behind his desk were a museum of assorted memorabilia – many items personally offered to him by the figures who signed them. A blown-up framed picture of my father-in-law posing with his partner in People Magazine was hanging on the wall. Untinted windows, which bore no additional window treatment, made up the walls of the office. As the tall windows nearly stretched from floor-to-ceiling, we deemed it "The Fishbowl."

Customers passed by The Fishbowl during our visits, and most would peer into his office windows at the magnificent spectacle. Some would take brief peeks but most would do something more along the lines of gawking. Usually, one of us would make eye contact with the passersby, at which time the customers would quickly look away.

My father-in-law was a tall and powerful man who demanded respect, and it was evident from the look on his face. He ruled his empire with a heavy-hand with everyone except me. Other managers, assumed we spoke of business in his office; the truth is we'd watch golf on his large TV. Obviously he worked, but he was the best at what he did, so, though he had a lot of work to do, it did not take him long to do it.

We discussed what we did that week or how hard we'd partied the night before. Due to his equally massive ego, I would usually listen to what *he* did that week, or what *he* did the night before. There was something about him, however, that was so intriguing. This *something* adequately justified his unhealthily narcissistic behavior. Besides, due to his vast resources, my stories sucked in comparison with his. Don't get it wrong; if he knew I needed him, there wasn't a better listener on the planet (there wasn't a better problem solver on the globe either).

"We" planned beachside vacations and Vegas trips, on which, we privately flew jets to 16,000 square-foot suites and first class hunting trips. On many such hunting trips, the males of the family traveled 1,500 miles away from home, only to shoot three birds each, then return home. On one occasion, we journeyed to Las Vegas just to eat dinner at a trendy spot and turned right around to fly straight back to Scottsdale only a few hours later.

I'd experienced an extravagant lifestyle but due to my powerful addiction, I'd not been able to enjoy most of it in an honorable and human way.

Conversations with John had grown more intense. During one such conversation, I agreed to join a waiting list and as with

Pollardo, John said, "You need to be prepared to fly at a moment's notice just in case another scheduled patient pussies out." During our conversations, John also informed me, "We need a certified check for the seven-grand we agreed upon prior."

So here was the plan: The treatments began on Mondays and ended on Sundays which was perfect for me since my start-up company was on auto-pilot at the moment, which left me free during the weekdays. I was to "wait for the last-minute call" from John, drop everything, and fly to San Diego. John himself would greet me at the bottom of the escalator, right outside the security checkpoint. We would then sneak through the Mexican border and drive down the Baja Coast to Rosarito, Mexico, where the infamous treatment would eventually take place.

My addiction had begun when my doctor prescribed Vicodin for a horrible shoulder injury, which I had earned in the gym. (Let's start with my accepting responsibility for this whole debacle; since that's out of the way): That became my routine – month-after-month — the doctor obliged. Each time, raising the dose as well as the frequency of ingestion until he had me hooked beyond escape; I recall the day of that ugly realization.

I remember going to bed without taking my "medicine." I laid there for twenty minutes, or so, before finally realizing I was wide-awake. In fact, it felt like I unknowingly had been injected with an ultra-powerful but chemically filthy stimulant. A high voltage current alternated through every limb of my body. My legs longed to run a marathon at full-sprint, without extending the rest of my body the courtesy of an invitation. A colony of earthworms had infested the space around my spinal cord, and were milling about the nerves, with no regard for my sanity, and that was only the beginning.

As I got to my feet and walked to the bathroom to take another pill, I began to realize the power of the dirty little compound. I'd heard about that sort of withdrawal from opiates such as heroin, but I was taking a doctor-prescribed medication…how can this be? I thought. That incident marked the first time I'd have to leave Katie in the middle of the night. I had left my prescription at a friend's house. It also marked the moment I had to tell my buddy, Jack, I had a problem. It was 2:00 am when I showed up sweating at Jack's house. Coincidentally, and unbeknownst to me, we shared that dirty little secret; Jack was also chemically dependent upon opiates.

As the efficacy of the drugs waned, I graduated from Vicodin to Percocet. I think "Doc" started me on the 10s and not long after, we'd moved on to the stronger ones. Soon I was all the way up to the oxys. I was prescribed both oxycodone and Oxycontin at once. When the volume of the real hard stuff ballooned, most pharmacies didn't even have the inventory to fill my generous scripts. There were days I went to a dozen drugstores flashing those blue tablet pages. Looks of horror were worn upon many of the pharmacy technicians' faces as they gazed upon my death defying problem.

On short notice, I was on the highest doses the federal law permitted the pharmaceutical manufacturers to produce. There was never a single educational session, lecture, X-ray film, MRI, or any other sort of treatment or measure taken.

My doctor's office was a joke; it was full of young people donning trendy clothes. Earphones were in many of their heads and some of the earphone-music made its way throughout the waiting room. There were crooked-hats with which one covered the top of one's ears, as well as one's head; most of them represented their favorite sports teams. Sports jerseys always seemed fashion-able, in combination with saggy pants.

I'm not mad at the youth or their fashion; I'm only pointing out that the doctor's "patients" were youthful in appearance. Some of the trends were pleasing to the eye and some of the vernacular pleasing to the ear; some of the loud music spoke to me as well. I have no opposition to any of those things, but there were no fresh amputees or apparent maladies there.

Frequent smoke-breaks were a common activity amongst the demographic of patients in the doctor's waiting room; group smoke breaks weren't unusual. One could watch the patients forge friendships and engage in all manner of grab-ass activities.

One time, I was in the doctor's waiting room for six hours and never once complained; it was 10 O'clock at night when I left. In those days, you left his office with your pills in your hand, he both prescribed and dispensed the poison. After several years, the Oxycontin was discontinued from my daily regimen. The doctor no longer wanted to prescribe it, "due to the overall negative stig-ma of the drug."

The doctor explained, "People are robbing pharmacies for them. They are murdering people, and that gives me bad feelings toward prescribing the medicine." Which is strange since....*All opiates are chemically the same drug*, just different strengths, mix-tures with other drugs, and physical offerings that release them more slowly into the user's bloodstream. My doctor continuously attempted to transition me to drugs such as Opana, Dilaudid, Mor-phine, and Suboxone, but even the transition between opiates in-cluded high levels of discomfort and withdrawal.

That shit-show had gone on for most of a decade. I won-dered if the medical board was finally applying pressure on him and his practice. The doctor was a nice enough guy. Unfortunately, he'd made a deal with the devil – as had I.

Monday I attended my scheduled doctor's appointment; it was time to refill my monthly prescription. But when I'd arrived, the doctor broke some bad news: Due to the doctor's overzealous prescription-writing practices, the Arizona Board of Osteopathic Examiners had indefinitely suspended his ability to prescribe prescription painkillers. Though that is not the story he had told me, I turned to the internet for those tender nuggets.

The doctor left me in the cold with no sort of an exit strategy. What timing, I thought! Now, without a legal opiate source, there was no turning back even if I had wanted to. The confiscation of the doctor's blue prescription pad, by the board felt final, but, at least, I had put a plan into place, even if it wasn't responsible, it was now in place.

It gave me some comfort that the doctor could no longer put others in harm's way. But, I couldn't help but feel compassion for all of the doctor's victims who had no plan and nowhere to turn after being cut off by the board from such a dangerous medicine. Those people, like me, were all just turned to the streets without as much as a pamphlet from the *medical* board, after taking heaps of that poison for years, if not decades.

I think the usual course of treatment here is traditional rehab followed by a lifetime of maintenance drugs such as those more-evil drugs: Subutex, Methadone, and Suboxone. These are all opium with a mask on, just like heroin and all the rest. Suboxone is the perfect opiate prescription for the doctor's commercial vacuum which occurs when a legal junkie's "aha moment" takes place. Suboxone fills the opiate receptor, preventing "dope-sickness," but doesn't get the junkie nearly as high as the "real thing" does. That may sound like a good thing, but Suboxone still makes one feel dead inside, and addicted to making doctors' and politicians' Mercedes payments. It is also common knowledge among users that Suboxone is a life-long commitment; it is chemically designed by the drug company to be impossible to stop using; that was the true value of the patent, not its *anti-addiction* properties.

Technology is a hell of a thing. Suboxone keeps the junkie even more addicted to opiates, and lining the halls of the medical empire, while giving the patient the illusion that he or she has quit using the opiates. But, Suboxone doesn't carry nearly as many of those unwanted *doctor-induced side-effects,* such as: robbing pharmacies, and cold, dead human beings with dried foam trailing from the corners of their mouths. A host of unwanted inconveniences can jeopardize the Evil Empire's activities; the industry of evil is a carefully staged fiasco, and the journey back to reality is a winding road of cryptic riddles.

The Osteopathic Board seemed to think my doctor's actions had required severe disciplinary measures. None of the authorities took any interest in my story, however. As if irresponsible prescription writing weren't enough, Doc was still able to practice medicine. Doc offered to write prescriptions for anything I wanted on my way out of his office: "just no opiates."

Once, when trying one of those "desperate-detox-methods" I told you about, I was three days into the anguish of the event when I felt a sudden pain. I had always had a high tolerance for pain, but hypersensitivity and the excruciating reality of a kidney-stone brought me to the ER. I was honest with the medical staff, informing them of my oxycodone problem; I spent that night in the ER, passing a kidney stone without any painkilling-agent whatsoever while detoxing from opiates.

The doctor insisted upon a urine sample; undoubtedly he wanted a drug test before he would begin any treatment. I told them, "I left my prescription in Mission Beach; we just got home." I didn't want to tell the doctor that I was home-detoxing, nor would he believed me. While crying in pain, I endured the doctor's lecture concerning my drug abuse. I passed the stone on my own; I think the doctor was attempting to teach me a lesson.

The doctor said, "See what happens when you're a drug addict? Tim, you need to seek help." My squirming made it hard to "sit still" for the lecture and the MRI, which came hours later. When the MRI results came, the stone had already "passed to the bladder." The doctor returned to my bedside holding a giant unnecessary syringe of morphine.

The ER doctor had the nurses who all showed me such empathy by his side (one of them, had even rubbed my bare feet while I contorted my body in pain). They all knew I was passing a stone. In fact, the male nurse who wheeled me in had diagnosed me from the car. Upon initially hearing my screams, he remarked, "I know what that is; I had one last month."

The female nurse who accompanied him responded, "YUP!"

The doctor shot me with the hypodermic, even though the pain was all over. He apologized profusely in front of his staff; the medical board didn't care about that either. That ignorant doctor had unknowingly held the unnecessary syringe with which he ruined that special chance for recovery. Resisting a giant, juicy, hypodermic full of your favorite antidote is hard; once again, I was left searching for the answer.

The night my doctor cut me off, the family and I ate Chinese, well, fast-food Chinese. My fortune-cookie-fortune read:

"Health and happiness are coming your way." Health and happiness had better come my way, I thought to myself. It would cost me twelve-thousand dollars to fill my prescription on the streets now that I'd been cut off by my doctor, that is, if I could find the volume of pills. Lately, my prescription had only been lasting a couple of weeks; I now looked to Mexico for my *health and happiness.*

Thursday morning, John called to explain, "Due to a cancellation, a bed opened up." That was quick, I thought. John advised me to pack warm clothes. I was to arrive at the San Diego airport on Monday morning, as earlier agreed upon. It was a brief call, as if John were preoccupied. I hung up and told Katie the good news.

The dreaded telephone call came only a couple days following the initial conversation with John, and a passport would've taken weeks to arrive; and, of course, I hadn't yet applied for one. Once again, I filed the information away in that dark cobweb-covered place where it was kept company by scores of regrets, misgivings, and unpleasantries. We kept the conversation light for both of our sakes. Katie and I stayed up late speaking of the possibilities, as well as the preparations we still needed to make.

Friday morning I motored to the dealership as fear cradled my body. When I arrived at work, it was the usual high-paced environment of meeting new people who weren't in a big rush to "sign the dotted line." The cautious consumers were scared of meeting me, but, one-by-one were tipped-over with words. The demanding nature of engaging the suspicious people loosened fear's tight grip, for now.

My brother-in-law, Dave, was new car director at the dealership. Dave, who happened to be one of my best friends, was a beastly alcoholic. While I don't understand alcoholism, I do understand the power of addiction. Dave had been hospitalized twice with cirrhosis of the liver. The cirrhosis had caused esophageal varices of the throat to burst, nearly causing him to bleed to death on both occasions; Dave also understood addiction.

He was a desk manager, as well as being new car director at our family car-store. On the following day, Saturday morning, while working the first deal of the day, I asked, "Hey, Dave, if there were a drug that you could take only once, and never crave another sip of alcohol again, would you take it?"

"What's the rub?"

I told him, "It's ten grand, treatment is in Mexico, and it's the most potent and disabling psychedelic known to man. You could have a grueling 72-hour trip, Dave. Would you do it?"

Dave responded immediately, "Fuck yes, I wouldn't think twice."

I'm not sure if it wasn't just a knee-jerk response, but it comforted me all-the-same. For me, it was an unexpected question, which I had asked out of fear – there was no intention to tell Dave my actual plans – but his provoking response impulsed me to blurt them out, regardless.

I continued by explaining to Dave, "Monday that's what I intend to do."

As he looked on in total disbelief, I discussed my itinerary with Dave. We also discussed my fear of it being a sick and dangerous scam. Dave was one of the smartest guys I knew, so I valued his opinion. Though being my brother-in-law, he was also my boss, so it was important that he knew what I was up to, in case things were to go bad.

Also, I could be too ill to go "right back to work" as the program had suggested. And, as mentioned prior, this was a matter of prime importance - my father-in-law could *NOT* become wise to what I was doing. It was then that I laid the groundwork for my cover-up story, which I would *have* to sell to the Old Man.

"I'll be traveling to Arkansas, Dave, just as I've done so many times prior. I'll be attending a corporate meeting in Little Rock to view a prototype of Phase I (*which our award had produced*). I'm expected at the meeting as it is, but I'll have to use PTO (Paid Time Off) days for treatment instead, Dave."

Not much more needed to be said between Dave and me since we both had great respect for one another, work, and otherwise.

What if this Ibogaine thing is crazy enough to work, I asked myself? But again, my better judgment took over, and my veins coursed with a healthy dose of adrenaline, forcing me to redirect my attention. It was time to say hello to those nice folks, trying to buy a car in sales-booth position 1-A; they'd already begun staring at me from 30 feet away. I snatched the worksheet from Dave and rushed in to visit with the customers, after which, I repeated the process time and-again for 13 hours until there were no more nervous consumers to mask my worries.

The following day was Sunday and the day brought more of the same; betwixt opiate fixation in the bathroom, via insufflation, I worked. One-by-one, we again transformed defensive people with ridiculously low offers into happy customers until the work weekend had decayed.

3.

Scaling The Walls

In grade school, hideous lies spewed from a foolish little member of the local police who paraded around campus in a dog costume. The goofy canine told his tiny captive-audience, "Marijuana will ruin your lives." He went on to add, "We will become addicted and suffer horrible physical consequences were *we* to try and quit" (WEED). I had begun smoking marijuana in my teens, smoking it regularly for several years after that, and as easily as I had started experimenting with the flower, I just stopped.

Admittedly, there were some mental side-effects to ceasing the use of marijuana, but they were nothing more than a bit of restlessness, and some vivid dreams. In one such dream, I walked through hell with a friend whom I had nearly lost to a gunshot at a party years earlier. A couple of nights of tormented sleep was the extent of marijuana withdrawal. It was no big deal. The inconvenience of quitting didn't outweigh the adventure marijuana had provided for the blissful stent.

As mentioned, the canine was a liar. And partially, it was those lies to which I owe my cavalier attitude toward the physically addictive, dark side of drugs. It was the lie itself that skewed my reality and opened the door to permanent chemical slavery. Marijuana wasn't the "gateway," it was the deception (about marijuana) which cracked the door to irresponsible experimentation with more-dangerous drugs.

The weekend before treatment was a blur, as were many of the past several years of being intimate partners with the demon who promoted my addiction. Keeping my mind busy during the thirty-six-hour work-weekend before Mexico helped ease my worries but I harbored a sense of impending doom that wouldn't subside, no matter how I occupied that time.

On Monday, I would board a jet and fly into the great unknown, and what I *did* know about the situation, I had heroically tried to forget. Everything pointed to a disaster, but I was weary from keeping up the ritual of addiction.

Sunday night after work, I still had nothing prepared for my epic journey, where one-way-or-the other, the nightmare would come to an end. The idea of Ibogaine being a horrible scam still resonated within. But my demise by the hand of an evil genius, who lured desperado Americans to their deaths in Mexico, was a far better life than continuing to live in a world where I could no longer feel emotion.

My demon had successfully taken over every facet of my life. He made me available for his every whim, disregarding my family and work schedules, and had no concern for my safety. He commanded me to frightening meetings with sketchy individuals who could only temporarily keep my demon's antics at bay.

My violent drug abuse had now reached a forte. I was consuming my monthly prescription of #380x30 mg oxycodone in less
than two weeks. (That is equivalent to 1900 of the little guys you
might've been given for your toothache the other day. That is not a
typo; it's nineteen hundred.) I found the remainder of my supply
on the streets. Just to stretch my pills to my next doctor's appointment, I was spending $350.00 a day, only to prevent being
sick. Getting "high" rarely happened anymore.

The financial expense alone prompted me to try heroin
since it was so much cheaper than the pills were on the street. I
bought a couple of grams of black tar heroin during the last few
months before Mexico. Once again, I realized the astonishing
power of oxycodone, after heroin did nothing toward satisfying my
need for oxy. (I wasn't willing to shoot-up; at least there was a line
I wouldn't cross, right?) And… After consuming all that dope, I
was still getting dope-sick.

I had slowly transformed myself from a regular
middle-class guy, into a dope junkie.

After I had finished packing on Sunday night,
Katie asked me, "Haven't you forgotten something?"

"I'm sure I have, Katie, but what?"

Katie insisted I locate the shadily photocopied birth certificate which my hippie parents had passed off as normal for so
many years. Maybe Katie grasped for hope so hard that she had
convinced herself I would somehow need the illegible, tattered
document? In the continued interest of my dramatic charade, I
defended the yellowed paper.

After another spontaneous bout of laughter, Katie made a
few more funny observations. "Whatever someone photocopied
here has been ripped, is mis-centered, illegible, and lacks the

state-required-seal, frequently legitimizing this sort of document."

Katie then laughed *while* crying. With a false sense of security, I tucked the tattered paper into my bag, mostly to appease Katie. Afterward, I medicated myself to sleep as I'd done thousands of times prior.

I woke up on Monday to an intense "what the fuck have I done!" sensation. There were only two pink pills left over, which I had illegally scored on the west side of town. The two pink 10 mg oxycodone tablets were from Dingo's the week prior, after the SNAFU with my prescription had taken place. (We'll get back to that.)

Those two pills were but a tranche of my usual morning dose. I crushed them on the bathroom counter, blew them up my nose, and reluctantly made-off for our SUV.

Ten years prior I would have told you that snorting pills was trashy-behavior, only exhibited by junkies. But with the medicine working less and less as time moved forward, it was a necessary evil; sniffing them makes the pills more bioavailable. For two years I'd been abusing them in that way, only wasting the occasional pill by popping it when I was unable to get to the washroom.

I had to get the pills from somewhere, right? That's where Dingo joins us in the story. I had purchased the handful of pink pills on the west side of town, at a run-down little apartment complex, from a little three-person family who lived there. (I had also met those winners through Jack, who seemed to have had quite an underground network.)

None of them had jobs, since they all had doctor-prescribed opiate prescriptions. G was their drug of choice. ("G" is glass or methamphetamine.) The family sold their pills to support their meth habit; they were always a complete mess.

I never knew what I'd see at Dingo's place, DVD-players, speakers, work-out-equipment, musical instruments; it was all there. The inventory was different with every visit, because, as it turned out, Dingo, was also quite the salesman, among other things. Many times while waiting for them to arise from the dark cave in which they slept all day, I'd see little kids pop-up from the mountains of stolen inventory. The lady of the house, "watched children," to earn extra money while they slept the previous party-nights off.

The reason I couldn't just buy more pills for my Mexico trip? I got into an altercation with Dingo, the man of the family, a small Mexican fellow with a crazy eye. I thought I had bought enough pills on that last trip to Dingo's – but, as mentioned, I had "mowed through them all." On that last trip to the west side, I made the mistake of telling Dingo about my upcoming travel plans, to which in a Spanish South Phoenix accent, he replied, "Hey, Mommy! Carry your big fat ass over here. We're take-een Tim to your cousin's house. COME-EAR-BITCH!"

A heavy-set, white lady, wearing a dirty nighty and an arti-ficially blonde, bird's-nest-hairdo, came barreling down the hall. "What, Mijo?" she yelled in a high-pitched, wobbly voice.

"Hey, Bitch. Tim here is going down south, to Mexico, to get clean off of our dope; he thinks he will be get-een clean by trip-peen on acid, aye. Let's take Tim to your cousin's and dig-him up some of that Loco Cactus. Then he won't have to go to Mexico for detox anymore, aye." "Ha, ha, ha, ha, ha!" the group cackled.

"We'll get his seven-grand, won't we Babe? You'll sweat a little, and it'll be all over," Dingo laughed. He continued his hys-

Page 39

terical laughing until swatting a big, red handprint onto his "Bitch's" ass.

"Aye, Poppy," his *bitch* squealed.

They then laughed me all the way out of the house.

"It's going to work; you wait and see. You're never getting another dirty-dollar from me," I assured the group.

"Hey look, you'll be back, Gringo. They always come back, don't they, Babe?"

"You will always be back," she agreed at the top of her lungs. That time, she made my eardrums vibrate and then ring. (Everyone followed me out.)

I held my middle finger high in the air as I walked out to my car. They laughed and pointed, muttering Spanish insults my whole way out of their dark, smelly apartment. I slammed the car door, which only muffled the excited mob when driving away. I felt like more than a dumb-shit.

So, that Monday morning, as Katie motored our way to the airport, her voiced concerns only enhanced the lies and overlooked facts that I had kept from her. With haste I deployed the mental "ear-muffs" routine, which I had developed long ago for combatting some of the crazy things she said.

That time, however, the mental "ear-muffs" routine was accompanied by my mentally chanting: "nyah, nyah, nyah, nyah. "I deployed this additional childish measure to ensure her fears didn't invade my psyche.

Phoenix Sky Harbor International Airport is where my wife dropped me off curbside. We both exited Katie's white Range Rover. I grabbed my bags and threw them to the ground. We embraced as if we would never see each other again. I saw fear deeply embedded in Katie's eyes, and she only tried to hide her fear by not speaking of it, but the look on her beautiful face held back nothing.

As Katie motored away, I navigated the ticket counter. Glimpsing back at our fleeing SUV, I saw Katie's head fall into her hands – her body draped over the steering wheel. I felt help-less leaving her.

Over the years, I had boarded a plane umpteen times due to the demands of my new business. There was only one significant difference this time. I was forced to go without those pills, since I had avoidably "mowed them down" over the weekend. The very nature of my problem forbade me to reserve enough oxy to enjoy a comfortable passage to Mexico.

I chose my usual aisle seat, toward the front of the jet, on the empty Monday-morning flight. After settling in, my old de-monic partner (dependency) wasn't happy. He wanted drugs, wanted them then, and wouldn't take NO for an answer. He also seemed to be privy to my break-up plans, which might have further convoluted the issue. Buckling in for the worst flight of my life, I took a deep breath.

Thank God! I'm the only one in the whole row, I thought to myself. But, before the fuselage door closed, a winded, middle-aged lady entered the plane. A deep whiff of jet-fuel fanned my nose as the door banged shut. N-o-o-o-o-o! I thought to myself. The jet-engines whistled. "Is this seat taken?" the out-of-breath lady attempted to whisper. With drama, she fanned herself madly, though she didn't appear to create much turbulence during her in-tense climax.

She occupied the middle seat next to me, leaving the win-dow-seat vacant. She was nice, but her being "winded," didn't last long, and her incessant-chatting guided me to our destination.

When we arrived on solid-tarmac in San Diego, I was overtly ill. The wheels touched the tarmac, and I powered-up my phone. There was a fresh text from John.

John's text read, "Waiting for you at arrivals."

I texted back, "I'm going into withdrawal, BAD."

John quickly responded by texting, "We'll make you comfortable just as soon as we get to the clinic."

I ducked into an airport bathroom stall and retrieved from my pocket 7-15 mg time-release morphine-pills. Eating the morphine pills was futile due to the extreme volume and potency of my drug of choice, but, at least, they temporarily prevented me from transforming into an immobile hunk-of-shit. I relieved myself, exited the bathroom, and headed for the "arrivals" curb.

Carefully negotiating the growing escalator step, I descended toward the "arrivals" deck. Upon my descent, I noticed a tall pretty-boy type at the base of the escalator. He favored Justin Timberlake and held a small, paper sign scribed in blue ball-point-pen (it was only a sheet of torn-out spiral notebook paper which had ripped on its way out of the spiral book). The abstract sign was hard to read until I approached John's personal space; when my nose nearly touched the sign, John finally mumbled, "Tim?"

John looked nothing like his picture on the internet, but I was far too dope-sick to overanalyze things; I nodded my head and followed his lead toward the parking area. Being extremely ill, at that point, I don't recall what we said on the way to John's car, but I do remember a level of comfort with the guy; he had a warm smile and a calm mood.

John opened the green driver-side door to his dated crossover, and opened it for himself; I approached the backseat door on the passenger side and opened it, as well. With my background in the car business, I instantly recognized that the vehicle had bald tires; the interior was ratty, and its surfaces plastered in dust and goo. The goo seemed to be a mix of dried coffee, soda, taco sauce, and the unidentifiable. Also, trash and belongings covered the interior surfaces of the unit. After opening the back passenger door, I couldn't make space for my bags, so I chucked them on top of the heap and slammed the back door. Then I slammed it again, this time with a great deal of extra force to compact the cargo within. It worked.

As I opened the front passenger door, I couldn't take a seat without again awkwardly addressing the pile. Normally, the host apologizes for a mess and fumbles around to make space for the passenger, but not in this case. Instantly I realized John was completely oblivious to my quandary, so I outstretched my left arm, lowered it to the seat, and raked the mess to the floorboard with the haste of a craps dealer.

After boarding the shitpile and melting into the seat, John threw the crossover into drive, and we sped away. Something unbalanced in the right front-wheel increased in frequency and vibration as we accelerated south toward Mexico: wop, wop, wop, wop, Wop, Wop, Wop, Wop, WOP, WOP, WOP, WOP, OP-OP-OP-OP,OPOPOPOP.

As we headed for the border John began some small talk, during which John loudly explained, "WE'RE HEADING TO A SHOPPING CENTER....TO MEET ANOTHER POOR SON-OF-A-BITCH....SUCH AS YOURSELF." John yelled over the road noise. "AFTER THAT, WE'LL HEAD TO THE BANK AND DEPOSIT YOUR CHECKS." I think I saw some spit hit the window that time. He was nearly impossible to hear over the car.

Suppressed fears crossed over the barrier from the subconscious to my conscious mind as John continued his loud but muffled dialogue. My mind began to drift as he did so and I could no longer play mental games with myself. If John were going to kill me, I might as well marinate in the experience, I thought to myself. It seemed like we drove forever as I ran through different scenarios in my head. Mentally I reviewed escape plan options. I also began to regret not coming better prepared, but, there just wasn't time.

We arrived at a San Diego strip mall type shopping center and parked. I started squirming in my seat while waiting for Wayne, the other poor son of a bitch such as myself. Ten minutes had passed and still no Wayne. John finally decided to call Wayne to ask his whereabouts. John spent some time on the phone before realizing that the older gentleman that had been in the car facing us, staring at us the whole time from the moment we'd pulled in, had been fucking Wayne. John was a bit of an air-head.

My patience was wearing thin, and my nerves became unsteady. John stepped out to meet Wayne and his wife, and then we were off to the bank. Wayne's wife must have shared my questions because she was going to follow us to the place also. She wanted to "meet everyone and see the location."

When at the bank, John again exited the vehicle, as did I, but mine wasn't as pretty. As if the whole thing were pre-programmed, I quickly sprung to my feet in a joint-jolting fashion and began to gallop like a marionette. My actions were erratic from joint pain, but I couldn't sit in his nasty car anymore. (John "sold everything" to get clean, so I surmised that, the *dating*-car must have been amongst… "everything.") Clumsily I followed John

Page 44

into the bank. John deposited our checks and proceeded to argue with the teller lady.

John and the bank teller lady disagreed on the "estimated three-day hold" on withdrawal which she had placed on the cashier's checks that Wayne and I had paid John for the treatment. (Now, the only time I waited for cashier's checks to clear for withdrawal was when I maintained an overdrawn account, as a younger man, and that was another scary sign.) I've made some crappy decisions in my time, but this one's a Duesy, I thought to myself.

As if the whole bank routine had never occurred, we were again walking and small-talking. John immediately went from angry to unaffected and smiley. After both re-boarding John's hoopty, we finally headed southbound again. When nearing the international border, I glanced over at John and noticed two nickel-sized burns on each arm. They were in the same spots on both sides. Each arm had one round brutal burn-scar on its top and another on its bottom just before the wrist. John picked at the scabs frequently while alternating back-and-forth between them, in a blatant attempt to charm my attention.

"FINE, I'LL BITE, JOHN. WERE YOU PLAYING AN INTENSE GAME OF CHICKEN?" I yelled over the concert of exhaust and shittiness.

John forced a laugh to begin his interpretation of the scars. "NO," John said. Another fake laugh escaped his diaphragm. Now in a deeper, more authoritative voice, and with a full breath, John explained over the howling car, "JESUS CHRIST WASN'T NAILED THROUGH THE PALMS, AS EVERYONE THINKS. THAT IS ACTUALLY A FALLACY. THEY NAILED HIM THROUGH THE ARMS, TOWARD THE WRIST, BETWEEN THE BONES OF THE ARM, OTHERWISE THE NAILS

Page 45

COULDN'T HAVE POSSIBLY SUPPORTED HIS ENTIRE BODYWEIGHT."

John finally stopped his blaring, and I used the balance of my questions quite sparingly, for fear it would start happening again.

It seemed this was a topic he loved discussing. He already had the burns but had re-scarred himself with a cigar several days prior, to "touch them up."

Being raised in a home in which "we" changed churches like most people changed their dirty underwear (at least my mother did and she dragged us to countless churches of countless denominations), I had no reason to believe in God, but, for some crazy reason, I still entertained the possibility. In any event, John's stigmata-bit seemed incredibly blasphemous, and a little bit dorky, to be honest.

One of the more notable spiritual-abortions I recall from my childhood? Okay, fine: While my mother was dragging us from church to church, my father took part in the Word of Faith movement in Farmer's Branch, Texas, in metropolitan Dallas. "Bob Tilton's" particular flavor of WOF spanned from the 80's to the 90's. Those Word of Faithers spent most of their time asking God for material gain but spent much time on "healing" as well. It's commonly referred to as the *Health & Wealth* message.

Bob's healing techniques included but were not limited to laying hands on the lame and yanking their walkers and canes from them on stage. Brother Bob demanded his flock function without them. Brother Bob Tilton had a massive collection of canes, walkers, wheelchairs, and a myriad of medical gizmos with which he had idly adorned the upper level of the sanctum like a big-game hunter.

He created a media circus upon which he built an empire. When I was a boy, I would puzzle: even if Bob were healing people, wouldn't the church have sent the medical widgets to people who could make good use of them, somewhere, where the great Bob wasn't? Even as a small boy, I could see through Bob's smokescreen.

Brother Bob's flavor of WOF also employed the ritual of speaking in other tongues, in which the "speaker," Brother Bob, in that case, chanted random syllables and transmitted the streaming drivel directly from his mouth to God's ears. I'm not judging anyone (besides Bob). I'm only sharing my personal perspective of his theatrics. At any rate, Bob was fluent in the "other tongues" dialect.

Brother Bob's rants on the heavenly hotline will be enjoyed on youtube.com for untold generations to come. Through shameless infomercial-style marketing, televangelist, Brother Bob, raked in nearly $80-million a year at the peak of his acting career. (My father religiously, *tithed, or—kicked-in—*10% of his gross monthly income while I was a child.)

Bob led the melee as my father took us kids to church every time the doors opened. Journalists allegedly discovered tons of soiled prayer requests in dumpsters behind the bank to which the envelopes had been permanently addressed beforehand by the church.

Brother Bob had advertised to "lay hands on, and pray for all prayer requests." Reportedly, the only thing in those envelopes that reached Brother Bob was the money, stripped from the envelopes by bank employees, again, allegedly. My father still defended Tilton, stating, "All men have moments of weakness."

Maybe that was Dad's sneaky way of not admitting to having been duped for nearly two decades.

John summed up his stigmata routine, stating: "I'm saving people by exorcising the demons of addiction. That's God's work; you cannot deny that." (Oh boy!) In closing, John added, "We are all small slivers of God himself."

Now knowing I rode shotgun with the Lord did nothing for my escalating ailment. With Wayne and his wife trailing close behind, we finally arrived at the Mexican border where we joined the great exodus which slowly funneled into several lines of cars and trucks. As we approached the border-patrol checkpoint, the bizarre realization of the self-destructive fiasco had begun to set-in. The denial of my very presence in Mexico was so uncanny that I'd caught myself wondering if I had teleported to the location like a corny *Doctor Who* episode. John's acting seemed equally weak.

I'd seen the evil recipe of gold, God, and desperate people unfold in a great finale of despair many times over; perhaps my formative "religious experience" had conditioned me to such times. The steady diet of the bizarre served with curiosity and gobs of danger caused me to live in the moment, reluctantly.

Now buckled into the ride, I made up my mind to roll-with-it, regardless of the consequences; I'd lived most of my life with that mentality. I'd grown up with four siblings who along with myself were dragged across the United States in a camper for two years by our parents, so I knew about risk and change.

When I was five, a "corporate gold mine scam," managed by my beloved grandfather and my "unsuspecting father" was dissolved by a federal grand jury. Gramps, proud and tight-lipped, refused to testify against anyone involved which resulted in prison time for Gramps. We sold our comfortable Glendale Arizona home to buy the 35-foot camper, and we lived in that trailer for a couple of years.

My parents made the living-room couch out into a bed every night, and the five of us children slept where the fifth-wheel hitch extends over the top of the truck-bed. A couple of carpeted steps led to the tiny room. My dad built two small sets of bunk beds, and one lined each side of the room in which my parents couldn't even stand. My baby sister had a pullout mattress on the floor; though, she would usually crawl in with her older sister.

Our parents had organized the whole outfit before we left, but, oh how that was quick to change. We pulled the camper behind a sparkly brown nineteen-seventy-something extended cab Ford truck within which the seven of us traveled. Before trucks had space behind the seats for passengers, the extended cab of pickup trucks were likely used for tools. We five kids rode in the compartment behind the seat for two years, as Dad dragged the wheeled-hovel down the highway while squandering our home-equity along the way.

Our parents had sold the camper trip idea to us kids as an "adventure." The folks spoke of travel to "Disneyland in Anaheim California," and "beautiful National Parks." The foray ended, however, in our settlement of the armpit of the USA and a bitter divorce. The "armpit-state" will remain unnamed and I'm sure you could say the same of any state under the wrong circumstances. You may already have one in mind. I will say this much, however: It is neither the great state of Arkansas nor the great state of Texas.

As an adult, I wondered if we didn't bounce from the scene only so Dad could enjoy what was left of his freedom before the "long-arm-of-the-law" reached out and bitch-slapped Dad. (Guilt simply by association with my Grandfather is what I'm implying here.)

The "fantastic adventure" was kicked-off with a trip to *Terminal Island, California*; that's where my defeated grandfather would call home for the next several years. As you may have already guessed, *Terminal Island* is a correctional facility.

I recall being six-years-old, walking through steel-barred gates, armed guards, and metal detectors, just to visit Gramps. Powerful tattooed reforming-criminals make a deep imprint on the impressionable mind. So does the idea of incarceration in general.

I still remember looking back at the great symbol of wrongdoing when leaving. Fearsome swollen men glared back icily from the multi-leveled complex, behind barred windows, as I thought loudly: Gramps is in there.

4.

"Jam Sandwiches"

Fresh out of cash, we landed in a trailer-park in the American South; Mom temporarily disappeared from our lives. Dad worked 14 to 18 hour days in the oilfield, which left us kids fending for ourselves. The principal called home confronting Dad for sending me to school in subfreezing temperatures in a T-shirt, holey jeans, and sneakers. Whatever happened during the awkward call sparked a trip to a box marked "lost and found," where I was caped with someone's piece-of-shit jacket; this was *my* idea of school shopping.

I told the principal, "I'm not even cold," to defend my father's honor. The art of lying to myself for mental insulation from shitty events was born. I can't recall the entirety of most school years, thanks to the tool.

When the color of my punch-ticket contrasted with that of my peers because I was on the "free lunch program," I went straight for the after-recess. When there was "lunch" to bring, it was brought in a brown-bag with a rotten brown banana to match. For the entree, a peanut butter and NO jelly sandwich—if the provisions were in stock.

There was usually some combination of total shittiness available for lunch, however. When we complained, dad always reminded us of that, mitigating his complicity in the neglect. When Dad was around, he'd josh with us saying, "If you were starving, you'd eat a jam sandwich, make yourself a jam sandwich. That's what we had to do," dad kidded.

"YAAAAAY!! What's a jam sandwich?" we'd ask.

"Take two pieces of plain bread and just...jam them together."

Only Dad laughed – loving words compared with his childhood. Dad rarely spoke of it. Dad was abused high-handedly by his step-father who allegedly had hung his loving father with his bare hands. "He wanted our mother; he murdered Lewis in cold blood," my aunt claimed. Being a variety of ages, we all fell for the jam sandwich bit on separate occasions; it was never funny to any of us kids – only to our Dad.

Consequently, I only remember eating the one jam sandwich for lunch. Come to think of it, I believe that was the last time I was in a school lunchroom for eating at all. It was also the last time my classmates made fun of my lunch; I was a hungry pupil, therefore, didn't give a rip about school.

While I admired Dad's faithfulness to what he believed, I can't help but wonder how many "jam sandwiches" were sacrificed for Brother Bob Tilton.

My peers carried contemporary Dukes of Hazzard and Star Wars lunch boxes from which they ate Ding-Dongs and

Twinkies. In addition, they had sandwiches, all clearly made with love, of beautifully carved meats and fresh veggies on deli-bread. Most of these were wasted because the healthy items usually went in the trash. I was hungry, swinging by myself on the playground when friends joined me. They usually held a loudly-colored juice-box with which they washed their lunch down. That was the end of the school dining experience for me. I'm surprised I recall that at all.

Here's why I love my little brother, Nathan: He, on the other hand, didn't give a fuck, never has: Nathan was a year younger than I. We five kids were all around that, in age difference. As it seems, our parents' religion encouraged breeding like hamsters: "Be fruitful and multiply," was implied during many of our mini bible-lessons.

There were no limits with our hippie parents. We watched Mom give live-birth to my baby sister, on a bed, in the house in Glendale. Mom used a midwife and had our sister at home; I was five.

Nathan and I crossed paths on many occasions at school. In our state, younger children who were gifted and older students who were average, often found themselves in the same class. And since Nathan was "gifted" and I was very "average," *we* sometimes landed in the same rooms. All the siblings were smart, but Nathan and Joey were both genius-level smart. They were talented artists as well. They could all color, draw, or paint anything drifting through their minds.

When Joey and I were only 18 and 17 respectively, we wrote a children's book together. It's entitled: *If I Were an Animal*, by Timothy Zigler. Joey illustrated the book and it is my only collaboration with Joey. Mom found it, polished it up, and had it published after we lost Joey.

Mom was a talented writer herself. The book was such a gift. But it still baffles me that two boys like us would bother with a project like that, even though I was one of them.

Any coupon or lunch voucher issued to Nathan was redeemed with frequency. Futilely, a Mason canning jar, full of camper tap-water was displayed at lunch with which Nathan washed-down his jam sandwiches. I don't know why he would have done that; the camper water tasted like rubber garden hose.

Looking back, this could have been Nathan's way of filling the trivial void of variety while filling the primal need for nourishment; the social aspect came secondarily for him.

Nathan's elegant shamelessness intrigued me. I hid behind the walls I'd built long ago. We kids all came from the same crappy ordeal, but all of us reacted differently to the same shitty stimuli. I admired Nathan's resourcefulness and thick skin, but that background is also when and how I had learned to fight. A bully pushed Nathan on the school-bus. He dropped his brown-bag and the Mason-jar inside busted; water and glass covered the floor.

The kids on the bus laughed at my brother and I snapped, mercilessly choking one of the children till he passed out. That was my move; my first line of defense (or offense) was to choke. We small kids worked out differences since there were no parents around.

We had all developed some passive dispatching technique. We didn't wish to hurt each-other. It came to that sometimes, but not often. We fought readily but loved one another dearly and still do.

The Mason jar ordeal landed me in the principal's office and came with a severe paddling. Corporal punishment was still rampant in the South; it never detoured me from getting the attention I needed though. The first "paddling" I ever received, at school anyhow, came from a great big African-American lady who went by the name of Mrs. Montgomery.

I'm sure she was a nice enough lady, as long as you weren't a student sitting in her class. My dad was quite the handy Punisher, too, but Mrs. Montgomery is the first one ever to knock me airborne with a paddle swing; and Dad, who worked construction, used the "bare butt method" and his weapon of choice was a kitchen cutting board.

Mrs. Montgomery wouldn't be the last, though. Coach Munk used a boat oar with holes drilled into it. He was our middle school principal. The boat oar whistled upon its approach, giving you some idea how the landing was going to feel. Most kids would sign the paddle and move on. I frequented Coach Munk's office so often that I had considered using a hash mark system next to my name to keep track of our many creepy dates.

Those paddlings became a form of currency with which I earned my superpowers. Now, I know, you may not believe that superpowers are real. But, allow me to explain. That same place in my mind where I locked all of those horrible memories was also a place I could temporarily visit sometimes. I could hide in there for the few seconds of the beating and then come out mentally unscathed.

That practice allowed me the freedom to do anything I wanted. Other kids lived in fear; I was my own boss. Other students had to go to class all of the time; if I didn't feel like going, or had something better to do, I just didn't go.

If I was in class and felt angst, stuck, like the most claustrophobic feeling in the world, I just stood up and walked out. If I were being picked on by a bully at school, I would wait for the right moment and pounce, regardless of the consequences.

At the height of my superhero days, I did just that. A large group of bullies surrounded me in gym class, after which one of them hit me across the back of the legs with a wooden ball bat.

They all began to laugh and point at me while my legs buckled and I grimaced in pain.

The timing wasn't right, so I ran out in front of the crowd when the bell that ended the class rang. I ducked into the boy's room until the group passed in front of me; I sneaked in behind them. When the kid found his locker, and now, only having a few of his friends around him, I knocked him out cold.

His friends quickly stepped up to his defense, but, after I assumed a defensive posture and invited them in, no one took me up on the offer. I backed away from the group and went about my business. When I arrived at my locker, I went to spin the dial on my combination lock and realized that my hand had become a claw.

It was a good thing that none of those punks stepped up because I had hit the kid with such force that I had snapped a bone in my hand, fouling the mechanics of the appendage. When I walked into the school office to see the school nurse, the boy was sitting there, holding an icepack to his head. I was holding my right hand with my left.

"That's him," the boy said while throwing his pointer finger all about.

"I need to go to the emergency room," I told coach Munk.

"Did you do this, son?"

"Yessir, I did, in self-defense. Well, kind of self-defense."

"You're not going anywhere until we handle your punishment, Tim," Munk yelled.

"Uh, you're wrong about that, Munk. My hand is broken, and you want to beat me? I'm leaving."

"You had better not leave this office, Mr. Zigler."

"Bye, Munk," I said while walking out of the school office.

After having my hand set at the ER, I went back to school with a cast on my hand and arm. Munk informed me that the kid was in the hospital and that my punishment would be "30 licks, or expulsion." I chose the thirty licks. The state laws only allowed Munk to issue three swats at a time so we made a schedule, which would serve us for the following ten school days. For those ten days, I would report to Munk's office to get beaten, once in the morning, noon, and we'd finish up our day with three more swift paddle swings in the afternoon.

Church giveaway hand-me-down centers are where we *shopped* for much of our school clothes. Nathan might've picked out a vest, and a tie; we siblings may have laughed. But no one else dared bully us; poor little fuckers were only being kids. They had no idea of the fury our little mob could unfurl on a moment's notice. (We must have appeared to have come from everywhere when one of us found trouble.)

Nathan's eccentricities left him in many-a-jam. Mostly I wound up with the upper-hand during the scuffles. He knew I had his back, so I think he baited unsuspecting bullies into his trap; the kid was smart. None-the-less, Nathan reminds me of the time *I* was choked out at the bus stop, or the time *I* got *my* face fucked-up. I bled all the way home from every orifice, and a front tooth dangled by a thread.

My whole life hung by the few threads holding that tooth into place. Things would have been far different for me without a front tooth in my head. God knows I wouldn't have had a replacement made. Dad looked to Brother Bob for all of our medical needs. Even as a young boy, I didn't believe Tilton could grow me a new tooth, despite his medical gizmo collection.

Nathan wound up being quite the sparring partner himself; Joey prevented me from being choked a couple of times; and my older sister kicked all of our butts when we got out of line.

We nomadically moved, re-hitching the 300 square foot camper almost religiously. Trailer park to depressing trailer park, we followed dad's dozer work in the oilfield. Though working brutal hours, Dad's earth-moving experience with Gramps had proven useful. I was Dad's "spotter," for backing the trailer into new locations. Many of the trailer hitchings occurred at night. We got pretty astute at connecting and leveling the mobile dwelling.

My older sister reminds me that Dad had enrolled us in more than thirteen schools in one year alone. At one such location, I faked an illness and cut school for the day; I just didn't feel like going. Of course, my father had left before the sun came up; he was such a hard-worker. After the kids had headed out for school, I cracked the shades and peeked through the windows. I was shocked to see that I was in the center of a *Love's Truck-Stop,* alone, until the others got "home" from school.

I remember feeling free and safe for the very first time. For once in my life, I just did something because I wanted to. I didn't have to don the walls of disguise that day, and I could drink my water and eat my jam sandwiches at home by myself, without judgment or ridicule. There wasn't the chaos of the siblings bickering as background noise or the violent trailer shaking when one gave chase to another. There was usually a combined scream, trailing behind them as they went.

It was glorious to be alone. All I could hear was the patter of my own bare feet, intentionally traversing the camper from window to window on the linoleum while following the ordinary people who carried on their average lives.

I loved my siblings but, MY GOD – late-night laundromat trips with mountains of shitty clothes, adventures of falling through creek ice, running home covered in leeches, let's not forget the time Joey and I found the double-barrel shotgun with its barrel stuck in the mud while swimming in the runoff creek behind the trailer park – these are the shareable stories.

Dad was so pissed-off at us. We thought he'd be happy since we'd found him a gun and cleaned it all up and everything. We couldn't understand why Dad also had to clean the gun only to march us right back down to the creek in the dark to get it all muddy again. Joey, being the oldest, was nominated to swim back to the bottom of the cesspool. Dad aimed the flashlight, Joey wore Dad's leather work gloves while clutching the shotgun. Joey kicked his legs wildly while throwing out as many one armed doggie-paddles as he could muster. Dad instructed Joey to "LODGE IT IN THERE AS HARD AS YOU CAN!"

Cracking the shades to the *real life* of truckers filling up and who knows what else is probably where I first learned to escape mentally.

There was no TV, but there was no need for one. I remained entertained while imagining why I couldn't have a "normal life" too. We kids raised each other, especially our baby sister. She was around three when the shit hit the fan. It is a good thing that children are mentally pliable. The parents couldn't provide much for us kids, but somehow we knew we were loved. That may be the variable that separates the over-achiever from the serial killer later on in life; it still sucks.

It was *Lord of The Flies*. I could fill volumes with my crappy childhood alone. Notwithstanding, I have a finite amount of time in which to tell you this story, so, I'm going to keep things moving along. And I would like to keep things light. That's as much of my childhood as I could bare to relive. I only thought I would give you a taste.

Dad loved us and did his best, but his back was against the wall. Mom loved us too, but I'm afraid she might have simply had enough; everyone has a breaking limit. Mom was just 16 when she married Dad, and in the eight years she'd been married to him, she'd had nearly as many children.

Later on in life, my childhood adversity rendered me uncommonly adaptable for the real world. All five of us siblings can't say the same, I'm afraid. My own crappy childhood had proven useful for car sales. I clowned upon the Dukes of Hazzard lunchbox-toting loafers. Their ant-ism led them in a single-file line to mediocrity.

I managed a team of salespeople who spanned from my age all the way up to senior citizens, at the tender age of 22. Beginning as a "green pea" salesman, I sold 18.5 cars; I made nine thousand dollars that one month. Not to sound like Gramps but that was a lot of money back then. My rare work ethic bonded Katie's father and me as fast friends; I moved up the ladder quickly.

As privileged as Katie's family was, her dad had also moved his family from a trailer-house in South Dakota to Arizona. He started as a car salesman on Camelback Road and wound up a dealer – it consumed most of his time. He rarely attended a softball game; he was too busy. Katie's mother, meanwhile, worked hard to get them where they were. Katie tells blood-curdling stories of running home from "Chester-the-Molester," and "staring through the crack under the front door" while waiting for her twin older siblings. Their mother was incredibly resourceful. The art of struggle isn't limited to the poor; it's just a different kind of conflict. I admired Katie's parents for fighting their way out of mediocrity; they both taught me a lot.

My father taught me a lot as well; I always admired his work ethic and tenacity. I can't imagine what he'd gone through emotionally during his long workdays; he put his head down and kept going though. He dug himself out of one of the lowest places an individual can be in. Only gramps knew of a worse existence, out of our family, at the time. Dad still loved my mother, but she was gone, and he did the best he could on his own; I respected that. Remember the "dark cobweb-covered place" I mentioned? That was the grand opening of the shit-hole. Instead, however, of the usual first ceremonial shovel-full of dirt, I tossed in the first heaping load of bullshit. That was when and where I cut the ribbon with oversized golden scissors.

Someone in the family claimed: "Gramps was pardoned by President Reagan," which may or may not have been true; either way, they released Gramps from prison We kids idolized our grandfather. Though being a devout Christian man, Gramps had changed, and prison stories had now become very familiar during visits with Gramps. He'd become a story-repeater in the end too.

Here's one: Gramps worked in the commissary and watched round security mirrors while "two-big-burly inmates sexually assaulted a weaker one with a Coke bottle." My sweet old grandmother always caught him and said, "Floren, you can't tell the grandchildren those stories."

To which Gramps usually replied, in a deep, gruff voice, "They need to know what the real world is like, Mary."

While fact checking this book, I revealed that the prison where Gramps was sentenced to serve his time, was NOT a co-ed prison, as I had always pictured in my little head. Sorry if that ruined things for you too; you're welcome if it didn't. Also, I remember being fascinated and bewildered that there would be drugs in a prison, much less, an island prison.

From the stories that Gramps had shared with us, you would've thought that place was a stinking spring break destination. Gramps said, "All of the other inmates used to refer laughingly to the joint as *Club Head.*"

Gramps claimed to have discovered the *'Philosopher's Stone'* with which he could: "transmute base metals into gold." Gramps secretly ushered me into the back room of his old mobile home where a Crown-Royal bag laid on the bed. He'd slip his big paw into that golden-roped, tasseled bag, then slowly he'd pull it back out to reveal a large, shiny bar of gold. Gramps displayed the bouillon that way many-times-over.

It happened to me as a child and even an adult, after they released Gramps from prison. Each time he showed me the gleaming wonder, I would pretend it was the first.

Later I discovered that Gramps had shown nearly all of us grandchildren the gold bar in the same way; we universally coined it: *Grampa Gold.* To this day, you could say "Grampa Gold" to anyone in the family and they would know what you said. My stern father explained, "That technique landed his sorry-ass in prison, and one of those investors was a grade-school teacher."

Father was an exemplary human being; Gramps was also, but more of a risk-taker. I liked to think that I had inherited a whole dichotomy of the two. (Gramps was on my mother's side of the family).

I asked Gramps questions about gold-mining, after which even more shiny wonders followed: He showed off rock-pulverizers, smelting-ovens, crucibles, gold nuggets and more. Grandma Mary didn't like my encouraging of Gramps, but I knew my limitations.

Gramps had a secret lab hidden underneath the trailer-house. I could never understand why we were always so poor, and Gramps had all that gold just lying around. His prison release came with the agreement to never own or sell his precious Grampa Gold again, which was probably why his lab was so "secret," though he never dared tell us that. When we were a little older, Dad confessed, "I hate to be the one to have to break this to you boys, but Grampa Gold is most likely only pinchbeck."

Dad recalled a scrapyard trip, during which Gramps had ordered Dad to collect an abundance of zinc, lead, and copper before one such "Investor Sales Meeting." Though he "couldn't be sure," he was always such an honest guy.

My little brother, Nathan, said, "Dad?"

"Yes, son?"

"Wouldn't Gramps need those particular items along with a few other sundries, if he were really making Grampa Gold?"

After that, Dad said, "Nathan, I suppose he would've also needed those things if he were indeed changing base metals into gold." Dad scratched his head and walked away. That fascinated us kids. Believe it or not, Dad never ruled out the idea that Gramps had made the gold either.

Often I thought Gramps had manufactured the "Philosopher's Stone" business, so as not to give us the idea that he was only breaking the law. Long after Gramps had died, my sweet Grandma Mary claims to have arranged gold sales between Gramps and his long-time mining-buddy, Melvin. Melvin was a weathered old-bird.

Melvin often loitered midday at the Grandparents' hill-top mobile-home manor; bending Gramps's ear and sipping Grams's precious sun tea. I can remember him scowling at all of us kids when we came around to hear whisperings between the two. Joey is the one who began to sensationalize the mystery, and we all just ran with it from there.

Gramps claimed to have had a "million-dollar-view" too, and he was right. We watched fireworks there on the Fourth of July, back in the good old days. A drive-in movie theater was down the mountain from them, and they were proud of that; pointing it out every time we'd visit. (We could always see the show clearly, but we couldn't hear it).

The grand-folks both fingered proudly down the mountain one final time at the large white rectangle when, much to their chagrin, an on-screen interracial couple were sweatily getting it on. As poor as Gramps's memory got in the end, he never made that mistake again.

After Gramps's death, Grandma bequeathed most of Gramps's notes and gold books to me; she knew my love of his mining activities. Grams and Gramps were always a refreshing break from the chaos of our nuclear family.

After my grandfather's incarceration, the Church revoked both his and my grandmother's memberships. I likened them to *Cool Kids Club Cards,* but for some crazy reason, what those people thought of her meant everything to my grandmother. That killed my grandmother, but they continued to attend services.

My grandparents were the most honorable human beings I had ever met, but their weighty ousting from the Church had left them to identify with Mom's family (us) the most. We shared memories of living on the fringes. They knew what it felt like to be rejected since my grandfather's funeral wasn't even allowed in the church.

Our aunts, uncles, and their kids were always stable. We were the only trash in the clan, the black sheep. Grams always mailed boxes of trendy used clothes after the cousins had grown out of them; our family didn't do as much growing as they did. There were five of them also. It was a well-balanced social experiment; there were even three boys and two girls in their family, just like ours.

Grams learned to clean houses for "rich people" after Grams and Gramps had lost everything. Some corduroy *OP Shorts,* in which I'd worn the blue cords on the fanny cheeks flat, came out of those boxes. And, that was before "OP" was available at your local Walmart.

I got "the good shit" first, being the tallest boy, always even taller than Joey, my older brother. Grams collected gently used merchandise, which found its way out of those "wealthy" households and was mailed into the camper as well.

We felt "The Cousins" looked-down-their-noses at us. We were like Cousin Eddie's family from the National Lampoon movies. But, maybe that feeling was just our insecurity at work.

The cousins weren't even allowed to have a television set when they were kids. I think it was against their religion. I'm sure their parents cringed at the thought of our melding. We would pull it down, adjust the rabbit ears, and watch the little set when the parents all left together. They were so fascinated with that little magic box.

My cousins' donation boxes had everything to do with my healthy self-esteem. I thank them for the hand-me-downs; it doesn't go unappreciated. Since the costumes had allowed me to hide our material short-comings, I fit in with everyone. Always in the American-South, the hand-me-downs were mostly trendier than whatever fashions were worn locally, which landed me in the more popular groups at school, but I got along with everyone.

Break-ups with more-popular girlfriends usually came within days of their birthday or a major holiday. No money circulated the camper-of-pain for fancy Valentine's Day gifts; I often felt sad about that.

Armed with the deadly skills of transformation, I became highly adaptable in any situation. I studied the way people spoke as well as their mannerisms. I had become an observer of people and their situations. I had to be to fit in. The culture varied everywhere, even if we were only a small town over from the last stop.

Grams, Gramps, and the cousins had lived the good life in Arizona for as long as I'd been alive. That made it convenient for our aunt and uncle to travel to California for their five kids' school shopping extravaganzas. That's why they always had "the good shit."

I moved my little family from Arkansas to Arizona when I was 21. Jessica was 2. We were still considered trash; I could feel the judgment. I was fresh out of the oil-field. We sold everything to move to Arizona.

I had a thick Southern accent at the time. I quickly discarded that; it was but another attempt to fit in. Come to think of it, the accent I spoke with before that was an attempt to fit in. I was born in Fort Wayne Indiana, and raised in Arizona; things were confusing. Moving my family to Arizona I thought would make me one of the cousins; but, it didn't. Maybe they did look down on us.

Grandma would ask Katie and me, "When are the two of you going to be married?"

(Katie and I have never really been married. Both of our first marriages were tragic enough not to hurry the formality.) Grandma's marriage question always followed my questioning of Aunt and Uncle's lack of interest in my family. I remember talking to my grandmother about her and Gramps having their church membership cards revoked.

I asked Grandma, "Grams, why do the ACs not forgive, if the entire Christian faith centers on forgiveness? Did Jesus not live amongst beggars and thieves? Did he not die for our sins? Why doesn't the AC church forgive? And, why don't they forgive old Gramps? Also, why were you lumped in and punished along with Gramps?" Grams never had answers to those questions, but I respected her tenacity and commitment to her beliefs.

I don't think Gramps was guilty of the crime for which he was convicted and sent to prison, but my grandparents' memberships were probably revoked even before the courts sent him to prison. In the minds of the elders, for certain; the church was judgmental.

I must say, though, he certainly did look the part of an old evil genius grandpa that just got out of prison, almost like a mob boss. Seriously, he looked like Al Capone; he wore parted hair, a five o'clock shadow, supple rosy lips, black horned-rim glasses, a thin sleeveless button-down shirt, a pair of "slacks," the scent of menthol liniment, and dress shoes, everywhere he went – EVERYWHERE.

Gramps was visiting in Arkansas right after my Mother settled there and he took me on a glorious trip to Walmart. My grandparents would always spend a couple of bucks on each of us when they came out, to make us feel special. One time Gramps ran into another nice old guy at Walmart, whom I recognized, but, I was never there with anyone overtly friendly enough to know that he was as well.

Somehow they got on the topic of old age. (I suppose it's just natural for a couple of ripe old guys – I'm already finding myself doing the same, at only forty.) My great-grandmother (Gramps's mom) had just turned 104 years old, and, of course, Gramps couldn't wait to share that with the codger. I will never forget this. Gramps said to the other old guy in a slow deep voice, "Mom just turned 104 years old; I don't know who would even want to be a 104 years old."

The sharp-tongued, white-haired devil quickly responded, "Well, Floren, probably someone who's 103 years old."

We all shared a good, clean, genuine laugh. (The more I thought about that over the years, the wiser it sounded to me.)

Back in Arizona, with my instant success at selling cars, I immediately bought my first house. Shortly after moving in, the Ex and I took a walk in the new neighborhood. We turned down a cul-de-sac, and there was the house in which Aunt and Uncle had raised the cousins.

Aunt and Uncle's house seemed so much smaller now. I was shocked because my house was even bigger than theirs. I couldn't believe it. Out of the entire city of Phoenix, I had randomly bought a house in my uncle's neighborhood. That made me feel like God had shone a little light on me everywhere I went.

Only the three of us lived in that big house when I was only 22; my wife, my older daughter and I. I thought I'd hit "the-big-time," finding myself doing carpet-angels in random rooms of my new house when I wasn't working. But, I worked a lot. After the crazy camper ride, that house made me so happy; it was my very own little country.

I don't think others appreciated things as much as I did. Sometimes during my off-days peddlers would appear at my double-doors. "Are your parents home?" they would ask. I would never dispute their implications – it was an easy way of getting rid of them – but that never got old.

Sadly, many years later, when our older daughter was eleven years old, poor old Gramps died in front of her and me. When Gramps was so weak, he couldn't muster another word, he'd groan, "Sarah, Sarah," followed by what might as well have been Greek sentences. My Grandma Mary explained, "Sarah was Gramps's younger sister, and she died in Gramps's arms when he was a boy."

When Gramps was in his state of delirium, he had a short conversation with my older daughter. All I remember is, as always, he called her "Angel."

"He hasn't spoken another word for over two days," Grams said. Gramps died only hours later.

Not long after the funeral, Melvin called me looking for Gramps's "books and notes." He had the personality of a Gila-Monster; I remember being intrigued by Melvin. Melvin was looking for something, which I offered to split. He would never say what the "something" was, and he terminated the call soon after it had begun. It was hard to tell what Melvin and Gramps had been up to for all of those years.

As mentioned, our grandparents' church was extremely strict, and my grandfather was no exception. Though, life had softened him up for the grandkids. Our parents married when Mom was 16 and Dad was in his twenties, and they made babies the whole time they were together. Maybe Mom was already on the run then. Gramps was a multi-millionaire, a pilot, and he had had an airplane hangar located directly behind the Ohio farmhouse, before he had lost it all. Wealth seemed important to the people of the church. One would always hear whisperings concerning individual church member's financial health, before being introduced to them; all of them did it.

My success had surpassed all of theirs, at the time but, later my oldest male cousin became the chief of neurosurgery at an Illinois hospital, and the oldest female cousin ended up marrying the richest kid in the church. Those pre-introduction financial-health-briefings at the cousins' church seemed to be paying off handsomely for their side of the family. Oh well, it felt good being on top while it lasted.

I kid, I'm proud of the cousins, but do you see what I mean about the social experiment, the contrast between the cousins and us? That always saddened me because all of my siblings were such special people, and they didn't get a fair shake. For some crazy reason, I always carried a lot of guilt, like I was responsible.

In the cousins' church, the men sat on one side of the church, and women sat on the other side. The cousins didn't believe in musical instruments, so they had the most beautiful harmony. They would only be caught caroling traditional hymns.

Gramps's favorite song was *The Old Rugged Cross*. Before old Gramps died, he must've already thought he was in heaven. Gramps was circled by a choir of his family while being serenaded by beautiful voices when he faded away from this world.

The aunts, uncles, and cousins, all sang hymns right in his living room, as he mustered a death-rattle, and his last breath escaped his chest like stale air from a big, old, poorly inflated balloon. I remember Gramps's jaw-dropping, leaving his mouth agape upon his demise. Afterward, an older couple arrived in a nondescript white cargo van and harvested Gramps; the vine had withered, but the fruit was alive, indeed.

When my sweet Grandma Mary died, it ended up the same way. But, this time, it happened at the hospital with my younger daughter present. She was three at the time. She begged to "go with, to see Gramma." I knew the end was nigh; I had already gotten the ugly phone call. My daughter cried and cried because she knew "Gramma" was sick and her mother wasn't home.

Katie's response, "Don't you dare take her there." (Katie was only trying to protect the young child. We had all been through so much as it was.)

My daughter and I cut and gathered the single sunflower that we'd grown ourselves in the backyard. We slid the flower stem into a slender vase and poured in some water. We only raised the one sunflower, for some reason. She would check on it every day.

The solitary sunflower was my younger daughter's pride and joy at the time. She ran into her room and returned holding a teddy-bear. "This is for Grams, and I'm ready to go now," she said. She held out her tender hand lastly, with her freshly changed shirt on backward, as my eyes welled-up in cohesive swells. The dams burst and a flash-flood ensued with no crying; I hit my face with my sleeve as I buckled her into the car seat.

The baby didn't biologically belong to me. The little blessing came into my life when she was only two. Her daddy was one of my dearest friends, and we had worked together since I was 21 years-old. He and Katie had also met at the car store. Katie was the receptionist, her ex and I were salespeople, and we were all great friends in the 90s.

Tragically, when the baby was only two, her father died in a horrible single-car accident on the way home from a lake party. Our mutual friends blamed me, but, Katie and I each had a clear conscience. While Katie and our "friends" were at his funeral service, I walked his car wreck site, gathering the shoes in which he'd lost his life; those are the circumstances under which Katie and I began our relationship.

With my 3-year-old in tow, we entered the automatic double-doors of the ICU. I could already hear the family choir singing Blessed-Assurance, in perfect harmony from down the hall.

Grandma's dining-tray was set up in front of her, so we sat her sunflower upon it.

I saw Grandma crack a small smile as she looked over the top of her oxygen mask and she looked scared. My daughter was on a mission, and I had no idea why.

"Take me to Gramma's head," my baby stated.

The family choir performed their usual set list that they had specially chosen for the occasion, so the songs were mostly about "going home to be with Jesus." I carried my baby to "Gramma's head." She tucked the bear into Grams's dying arms.

Finally, my baby asked Grandma her big question: "Will you please tell my Daddy hello when you get to heaven, Gramma?" she politely asked.

Grandma said "Yes, of course, honey." Those were the last words Grandma Mary spoke.

The RN on duty in the ICU came into Grandma's room after it was all over and shared with us her perspective on the episode. "I've seen a lot of people's passings, but Mary's may have been the most beautiful thing I've ever witnessed – anywhere." (They truly are a remarkable clan.)

After Grams had died, the Church reissued Grandmother's membership-card. I remember wanting to vomit in my mouth since it was too little, too late. That's all she had ever wanted. Due to her last-minute clemency, Grandma's funeral took place in that judgmental establishment. For a lot of my life, Grams and Gramps were the only consistency I had had.

5.

Supertramp-ing

The sea of cars and trucks slowly trickled through the checkpoint while waiting to be hassled by the officers who held cartoon-sized machine guns. Their chests seemed three-feet-thick. I asked John, "Were you ever searched when entering Mexico?"

To which John replied, "No, never."

Within minutes, the pair of us were shaken down and perched on a curb.

They tore apart the crossover and blended the contents of my neatly packed bag with John's mess. Until being "made comfortable," my things would have to jostle about John's dated crossover as we pressed on. Although ill and disheveled, I was shocked at the ease with which I'd entered Mexico with little documentation.

Tijuana, Mexico, is affectionately known to the locals as "T-J," and when one initially arrives in TJ, one will first notice an enormous concrete canal. I had visited the more Americanized vacation destinations in Mexico but never before had I witnessed the third-world humanitarian disaster that is the Tijuana Canal. It is my understanding that TJ is a progressive city in Mexico too and that is extremely frightening.

"TIJUANA, MEXICO, IS THE BIRTHPLACE OF THE WORLD FAMOUS CAESAR SALAD! TJ HAS MADE MANY UNPARALLELED CONTRIBUTIONS TO THE RECORD OF HUMANKIND!" John informed!

John might have offered that tidbit to muse my concern away from what grew closer on our right. There were dirty, poor people everywhere, in and around the canal. The individuals moved as ants in a massive colony, each of whom had a job to perform. Except in that case, instead of leaves and dead insects, they dragged dirty mattresses and large chunks of garbage.

The ones closest to the vehicle begged for cigarettes and money. Many of them were double amputees, scooting about using their hands. I don't know why, but it mesmerized me. I knew Americans had it good in comparison to the rest of the world, but, this was a mer noire of people walking in sewer water.

Though ill, I was fascinated by the canal. I couldn't look away, even for a second; I imagined what individuals were doing there, and what activities filled their day. Again, I was enthralled with people – all people.

I'm ashamed to admit that the unusual pageant made me feel better, and part of the attraction was seeing people who were almost as miserable as I was. (I know it sounds haughty but don't give up on me.)

Trading places with any of them for two months would be better than what I was on my way to undergo, I thought. As I watched the jumbo Mexican-flag flow by my window, the gross realization that we weren't in America anymore began to set-in.

From beautiful San Diego California, it is only a 30-minute drive to Tijuana, but, I swear, the second you cross the border, everything is different. That isn't just my arrogant American point of view either. Even the locals will tell you: "The second you cross the border, it just smells different."

Since my sense of smell hasn't worked right for years due to insufflation. I'd have to take their words for the extent of it. It's one of the most bizarre anomalies I'd ever witnessed.

With the prospect of being "made comfortable" growing closer, we slipped down Mexico's version of the PCH (Pacific Coast Highway), and the international logistical challenges dwindled. John and I became more acquainted. During most of the drive, stories were told over the car noise by John while frequent incoming calls from potential victims were taken. After the calls ended and our conversation picked back up, John's personality shifted back to cool guy mode.

This guy had adapted the same skills I had adapted for surviving harsh circumstances. I figured him to be from a large family. He expounded his ideas in the same monotone he had used initially to lure me into his medical tourist-trap when on the phone. John took the calls and I appreciated his sales skills; sales are always the same wherever you go, and John was proof of that.

When on the phone with these "diseased individuals," he used the soft empathetic voice of a funeral-home director. I wanted to like the guy – I did – he was good-natured and had a great sense of humor. John had completely lost the aurora of an addiction counselor and now exuded an excellent drug-buddy quality.

We found common ground in that the landscape in Northern Baja California, Mexico, reminded me of a movie directed by Sean Penn: Jon Krakauer's chronicle of the Christopher McCand-

Page 77

less story. McCandless loathed and isolated himself from society during his journey *Into The Wild* and a shitty childhood inspired the adventure; McCandless and I had that one in common.

The only difference is, Chris went Into the Wild and I fled into the chemical wild, but we both escaped. I had just fled in a different way. Regardless, we both eventually found ourselves in Baja California, Mexico. Since John had also been treated in Mexico and now made it his home, he felt the spirit of McCandless was lent to him as well.

True story: McCandless fled the United States to the Southwest, also with no passport. He spent some time in Mexico and part of the movie was set in the area. The film included an intoxicating soundtrack written and performed by Eddie Vedder. After remembering the ending to that story, I again fell silent.

We could now see the ocean as we vibrated our way down the coastline of *La Playa en Tijuana* (the beach in Tijuana) in John's dated green crossover. As exposure to the coast unfolded, a vibrant, colorful, touristy scene, was slowly being sketched into a seaside paradise, with fisherman in colorful wooden boats, seagulls, surf, and pelicans.

The homes along *La Playa en Tijuana*, also, in no way resembled the houses just north of there, along the same exact coastline. In contrast, these homes paled in comparison to those in say, La Jolla, but seemed considerably more livable than those of Tijuana. There were half-built concrete structures with exposed rebar and cinder-blocks everywhere.

The partially unfinished monster-dwellings were sprinkled in every beach neighborhood, even the "nicer" ones. John replied after bringing that to his attention, "THESE ARE NORTHERN MEXICO'S VERSION OF SOUTHERN CALIFORNIA CITIES

AND FOR MEXICO, THEY ARE REMARKABLY COS-MOPOLITAN!"

The ocean's comfort calmed my nerves, for a while. The ocean had a therapeutic quality for me, as it did for so many others. Two of the only promises kept by my parents on the camper dash were: Disneyland, and the beach. That was my first ocean experience through these eyes, and it was magical. Our last dance with childhood bliss occurred on that empty, cold winter morning on Huntington Beach. Prison rosters don't care about peak seasons at places like Disneyland or the beach. It was so chilly on that beach, and we were the only camper at the beachside RV Park. I can still see my siblings and me in slow motion under gray skies enjoying our last glimpse of innocence.

Anymore, mostly, when visiting the same Southern California strip of coastline, it was for vacationing at the beach house with Katie's family on the Fourth-of-July. That had crossed my mind several times since touching down in San Diego, which caused me to resent that this would NOT be one of those fun family trips I had been pondering about. The heaviness of helplessness covered me. Finally, John said to me, "SEE THAT YELLOW HOUSE AT THE END OF THE GATED COMMUNITY? THAT'S WHERE WE'RE GOING!"

The brakes squealed, he cut a hard-right, and ground his poor warped rotors to a brief stop. Down a steep drive, we again slowly coasted as he left off the brake only. We again slid to a stop just short of hitting something after another solid pedal mashing. My vision was now completely blurred, and my stomach was uneasy.

"MOTHERFUCKER!" John shouted. "THE GATE'S FUCKING CLOSED AGAIN!"

John bailed from the crossover, made-off running, and jumped the fence which surrounded the single row of houses lining the rocky coast. The crossover sputtered, popped, vibrated, and missed during John's track performance; he sprinted up the private road, past the row of houses until arriving at the yellow house on the far North end.

Suddenly, the gates of heaven automatically opened right before my blurry eyes, even if it was only a rusty gate with lawn-mower wheels attached. Finally, I was within-visual-range of the yellow building holding the antidote for my malady. Winded, John made another hard-right, coasting the remainder of the driveway, and once more brought the nasty green wreck to a stop.

Out of the dark open doorway of the house came a silhou-ette. Squealing power-steering, vibrating, rattling, popping, metal-grinding, over-yelling, gas huffing, smoking under the hood, and all forms of undesirable happenings instantly expired. Except for the gas fumes and the smoking, which escaped the hood-line and continued their subtle waltz in the coastal breeze.

Slowly I removed myself from John's car, my knees buck-led, and I vomited profusely. I turned toward two more silhouettes that snuck up behind me. One of them began to speak. "Oh, you're sick, aren't you b-u-u-u-u-u-d?" Wayne asked.

His voice was a strange fusion of Thurston Howell III's ar-rogant-draw and the bubbly cadence of a valley-girl. Transferring the mess from the mouth to the hand with an arm motion, I coaxed no handshake. Wayne said, "Hi, I'm Wayne, and this is my wife, Christi."

I replied, "Hello," and turned toward the dark entryway of the beach-house, making a conscious effort to move my feet.

Come on, Tim – one-foot-in-front-of-the-other – I thought. When I neared the door, the dark moving object approached me.

Confused, I stopped, and the object bumped me as I felt a warm, lotioned arm slither around my neck. The arm felt soft and bore the odor of a flower bouquet, beguiling the scent of stale gasoline and fish.

Struggling to focus my eyes, I fixed upon a beautiful, twinkly-eyed, middle-aged Mexican angel. She wore blue scrubs and a contrasting scarf which complimented her scrubs nicely. I released my intense focus, and my eyes relaxed into a blur again. She embraced me with a soft voice and a thick Mexican accent when she whispered in my ear, "You are sick?"

"Yes," I replied.

To my dismay, she kissed me on my mouth's corner from which she'd watched me wipe puke with my hand. Our arms inter-locked as she led us through the front door.

When walking, she said, "I'm Jessica, and I'll be your day-nurse."

From out of my fog, I mustered a smile and said, "My daughter's name is Jessica, and she's also a nurse."

Jessica smiled. My smile quickly vaporized as the nurse helped me to a chair at a kitchen table that overlooked our ocean through a large, glass window, behind the table. I asked Jessica another question, she merely smiled. There was no reply; I just assumed that Jessica spoke very little English.

The smells and sounds of cooking could be heard and sensed throughout the community, *it seemed*. Whoever did so, drummed upon pots and pans as if the volume and frequency alone would increase their job security. It was maddening. Wayne and Christi, Wayne's wife, took seats next to me at the kitchen table while I rested my head on it. Jessica gathered some Kleenex for my pouring face as I detected John in converse with another unfamiliar voice.

The strange voice introduced himself as, "Grady, the owner."

"These guys are dope-sick, Grady," John stated.

"Sick already? They just got here," Grady observed.

"I know, man. But I promised Tim we'd help, and I just found out Wayne's also getting dope-sick."

(In the car biz we call this overcommitting and under-delivering. Except, the way they're doing it is probably a good way to get yourself hurt or killed with the kind of desperate train wrecks of human beings that come barreling through this oceanside manor. Having managed car salespeople and managers for two decades, I know. They are the same people who would be rolling into this B&B; people like me but not as nice.)

John and Grady disappeared into a room nearby and slammed the door shut behind them. They raised their voices as differences between them were chipped away. I remember feeling extremely uncomfortable with the whole situation but several minutes after the scolding, the two resurfaced. Grady handed both Wayne and me a brown, Mexican-made, sixty-milligram Oxycontin. He didn't seem happy about it though.

Instantly, I tossed the tablet in my mouth and chewed it like a skittle. Little-by-little, over the next thirty minutes, my body relaxed and the violent drumming in my head ceased. When my eyes came back into focus, I looked around to assess my surroundings.

Just Thursday, John had called, and I had worked 36-hours in three days with no time to even think and then this roller coaster. Clearly it was going to be a long week, I thought. Staff members gathered around us at the kitchen table and things around me started to come into focus. Craning my neck almost backward to bring the ocean into view, I noticed that the house rested on a bluff overlooking the beautiful Pacific. What appeared as a little single-level house from the front, had now opened up into a sprawling concrete mansion in the back; the levels seemed to pour down the bluff.

Once more, I laid my head on the kitchen table, until, NOT SICK. I raised my head and scanned the house; it seemed nice at first glance. Upon further inspection, however, it was sparsely decorated, and there were small imperfections in its craftsmanship. It was mammoth and super-cool. Mexican helpers loaded the fridge, filled the cabinets with cookware and cooked all at the same time in the wide-open kitchen.

Nurse Jessica arrived at the kitchen table holding a large cardboard box from which she produced an analog scale. She placed the scale on the floor and asked me to step onto it. Wayne and I weighed-in publicly like prize fighters, and our vitals were monitored and recorded. John produced two green folders, which he slammed on the kitchen table in front of Wayne and me. "Sorry, I didn't mean to do that," John apologized. (He seemed to be under some duress due to his verbal with Grady.)

Wayne and I thumbed through the legal pages, expeditiously scanning the policies and procedures at Ibogaine University. I could tell, Wayne too had had some contract experience. He licked his thumb and index-finger and burned right through the amateurish legal-disclosures.

Once again, there were typos.

It was nice having a reasonable, more mature person with whom to share the experience. Wayne seemed grounded, and I could tell from the little conversation between us that he was intelligent.

Most procedures contained your boilerplate liability-limiting language. A few things were particularly noteworthy, however:

First: "I understand that there is a risk of death associated with Ibogaine treatment."

Second: "Once I sign this document, I assume the risk of death associated with Ibogaine-detox."

The ass-kicker though: "Upon signing this agreement, I understand that there is a no-turning-back policy. We will administer the treatment, one way or another."

Quickly, I flipped to the back page to sign and date the document. I noticed Wayne doing the same, after which he slammed the folder shut and said, "We're all fucked now."

Though being funny, Wayne was right. There was no point in even reading anything else. We had officially signed our rights away in a third-world country. I had the feeling we had already made the mind-altering commitment, even before we signed the docs.

Grady abruptly interrupted, "Oh shit, Jessica, where's the paper I'm supposed to read every time? It was here somewhere." Beads of sweat now condensed on Grady's forehead. Speaking Spanish, Grady communicated more loudly through a litany of impatient-syllables. After lecturing Jessica, the two rushed back out to the garage.

Wayne and I enjoyed some more conversation. We noticed the Mexican helpers carrying in more boxes of household items and placing them throughout the house. We just sat and watched them for a while. They unpacked the boxes and decorated the house with astounding efficiency. Wayne's wife, Christi, excused herself from the table, then went out for a cigarette. After introducing myself more formally to Wayne, I gave him a truncated version of my drug story since I felt somewhat better. We still sat at the kitchen table.

"Why…that's quite the story. Tim, you are refreshing. I was afraid I'd be here with a bunch of punks."

"You have no idea, Wayne."

Wayne shared his story. "I'm a contractor in San Diego – have been for decades and the area has been quite good to me. I also own several rental properties in the beach cities, mainly, multi-unit dwellings along the Mission Beach boardwalk. They are quite the blessing."

"Wow, Wayne—right on—good for you. We summer there for a week each year, so I know what those babies are worth."

"Well, I know," Wayne downplayed. "But they were part of an inheritance from Dad."

"Oh, what did he do, Wayne?"

"Well, my father was a surgeon in San Diego for a half-century. He was also an animal of an opiate addict. That's how he died, and he was in his eighties."

"No way!"

"Yeah, Tim, right before he passed, I found him tying off on the floor of his house. He'd been an IV-heroin slash Demerol addict for most of our lives. I've also been a user for quite some time. I'm up to a thousand milligrams of Oxy per day this go-round, and it's been going on for the better part of a year now.

Next stop heroin and I should know. I've seen me do it, several times. I don't want that again," Wayne admitted.

"Whoa, Wayne."

"Yeah, I know, right? It all began with a giant Oxycodone script, following knee surgery. Like everyone else, the axe-head eventually flew off-the-handle. I didn't even know what pills were before that surgery. Dope doesn't care why you started. I take full responsibility, Tim. However, the doctor nudged me along, you know?

"Opiates took control of my life; I've struggled with them off-and-on ever since. I'm the kind of guy who'll use for eight months-or-so. Then, I go through living hell only to continue the cycle, to no end. On the internet, I read: 'Ibogaine can reset the brain to its pre-addicted state,'" Wayne stated.

"That's what it says," I added. I was still quite skeptical.

"I certainly hope that's true because I don't believe I'll last as long as my father did," Wayne sighed.

Online, the "Ibogaine University" facility was an all-white hospital-type setting, and we were in a residential structure which in no way resembled those pictures. Also, the place was supposedly in Rosarito; we seemed to have never left Tijuana. Though Wayne and I enjoyed a couple of minutes of privacy, neither one of us addressed the glaring disparities that hid in the furrows of our faces or the cries for help that had retreated to our eyes.

Grady and Jessica returned to the kitchen table. They both remained standing, Wayne and I remained seated, John was gone. (Surely John must have been pouting somewhere over the dispute he and Grady had had.)

Grady was a husky fellow who also carried a significant amount of extra girth. He had one of those horizontal wrinkles between his eyes where the bridge of his nose met his forehead and he had an overbite. Grady had a thick black fro and his fro-line only measured about an inch between it and his eyebrow; you heard right, singular eyebrow.

Grady was clearly Hispanic, which did not explain his name. He used a light Southern American-accent when engaging in English and when barking out Spanish orders to the many workers. Grady was the *Yang* to John's *Yin*.

John, the salesman, developed a comfort level to lure in the unsuspecting consumer and Grady was the guy who brought the buyer back to reality. Grady seemed to be the enforcer, the closer. (At the store, we call this "good cop, bad cop.")

Now sweating profusely, Grady clutched the wrinkled papers tightly in his angry hands while reviewing verbal amendments to the legal form we had signed earlier. As Grady spoke sternly, the help continued their swift decorating-effort which we all noticed but still chose to ignore. At that point I had the awful feeling the location was being staged right before our eyes. Grady closed his speech with a harsh warning, "DO NOT LEAVE THE COMPOUND!"

As the meeting came to a close, Grady finished with, "You are now free to move about the premises, *not the country.*"

I walked the long hallway and exited the front door, the one through which I had initially entered the yellow structure. There was a U-Haul-type box truck parked in front. The backdoor was rolled up and the ramp extended. Sun-fading could be seen around where the vinyl advertising letters had once been. Those read, well, U-Haul. The truck wasn't old either, so I imagined it to have been swiped recently in Southern California and brought over illegally, somehow.

The many Mexican-workers quickly made their way up and down the ramp clutching fake plants, medical equipment, and other household items that someone had haphazardly previously piled in the truck. There were more workers feverishly making repairs to the house.

I looked at the dwelling from the front and noticed rusty bars covering every window, all the doors, and surrounding the entire front porch of the structure. A remote control "clicker" was attached to an old leather strap that dangled from the peeling, rusty metal cage that surrounded the entrance of the home. I instantly knew that it controlled the gate to the small community.

The number of people and the efficiency with which they all appeared to operate was daunting and suggested extensive moving experience. After the crew had removed the items from the box truck, the crew placed many of the items in another hefty pile on the garage floor.

Re-entering the dwelling, I walked through the house, back to the dining room where the reception and orientation had taken place. The large glass dining-room window had an open view of the porch as well as the ocean and dark rocky islands. I exited through the glass sliding door that led to the porch.

I could also see in from the porch, since there were no curtains or shades to block the infinite view. I was at the very edge of the world where our domain meets the universe. Being on a bluff with a Godly vantage-point that had the islands as a backdrop may have helped push that brushstroke across my mind. The glass door resisted, but I forced it to shut behind me.

Yellow and white, glossy Mexican tile covered the porch floor. The handrails were decorative molded-concrete with vertical pillars, typical of the Mexican coastline. A large green netted hammock reached between two of the concrete support columns. While absorbing the ocean with eyes-closed, the cool ocean breeze met my face with a slight sting, and I noticed that the pill was working more.

The two small firmly placed islands seemed close to us. I don't know – maybe seven to nine miles from our location. (Exercising my powers of observation would prove simple there.) Fisherman and boats of all sorts were buzzing around, military even. It was a perfect setting to fall in love with the trivialities of a foreign people just grinding out an existence, but, I suppose, I was the alien there. I turned to see the sliding-glass door screech back open, and Wayne stepped out to join me.

"The Coronado Islands, or Las Islas Coronado, if we're proper," Wayne educated me with a long skinny pointed-finger pointing in their general direction and speaking with an authoritative tone.

Though white in appearance, Wayne spoke excellent Spanish, again, like a valley-girl from *Gilligan's Island.*

"The only Coronado Island I am aware of is off the San Diego coast and has a bridge connection."

"Before Katie's family began vacationing in *Mission Beach,* the *Hotel Del Coronado* was where we would take the kids in the summers to get away from the heat," I replied.

"Ah, yes, the *Silver Streak.* I have so many fond memories there."

I didn't know what "Silver Streak," meant. I wasn't going to ask, either. Maybe I'd already said enough because more pontification ensued as Wayne again pointed at the waters just north of the islands. "That's the imaginary international border that separates Mexico from the US. RIGHT THERE." Wayne performed a more spastic finger waving as if I could see the damned thing in the water, and there was danger of it getting away as he continued, "I was born and raised in San Diego, California. This stretch of Mexican beach was among my stomping grounds as a young adult."

I enjoyed Wayne's history lesson tremendously but I had become far too wilted for the impromptu tutorial.

Wayne recounted wild stories of driving down the coast on surf-expeditions. His descriptions of surf-safaris included crazy partying and the precarious predicaments his surf-party had encountered while doing so. I said little in response to Wayne's history lesson and after a brief pause, we both awkwardly began speaking at the same time. I yielded to Wayne's query when he asked," Aren't you nervous about this whole thing, Tim?"

"Yes, very."

"This is all very strange, right?" Wayne asked.

"Uh yeah! You bet your ass it is."

We muscled the heavy sliding glass door back open and returned inside—the door seemed to be off its track. We both had questions, I could tell. But, perhaps, neither one of us had wanted the answers to them yet.

6.

The Starck Reality About Joey's Wookies

After walking in through the back sliding-glass door, two jovial women came loudly strolling in through the front door.

The older woman appeared to be in her mid-forties, was a tiny little thing, and couldn't have weighed more than a hundred pounds. She had a Euro-Spanish-type accent, which certainly wasn't a local variety of the Latin-American slang dialect of Spanish. I couldn't understand any of it.

The younger one, who appeared to be in her mid-twenties, was a tall beautiful blonde. She instantly detected Wayne and me, who again were sitting at the dining-room table. Tiffany loudly asked, "WHAT'S UP, MY BITCHES?" (There was no formality, no introduction, no nothing. I felt like I was at a high school house party.)

John, who now sat in the adjacent living room, rolled his eyes with a fake smile that quickly morphed into a look of concern. Then, while walking toward Wayne and me, the young blonde asked, "Are you two here for the treatment?"

The two girls looked at each other and laughed immaturely, like the whole thing were a joke. John loudly interjected, "Come-on, come-on, let's act normal, girls."

John invited Wayne and me into the living room and the girls were quick to take seats with the three of us. The five of us now occupied recently placed white leather couches that were located around a more-recently-placed big screen TV. The girls made it painfully obvious that they were bored.

Wayne asked, "Are you two ladies here for Ibogaine treatment?"

"Yes, yes, the girls just went through the entire treatment process," John blurted out.

Part of me wanted to become optimistic since these women quite obviously didn't show clear signs of detox, but the other part of me knew things just didn't add up there. John stood before us and broke down the activities list. "Okay, Wayne and Tim, here in a bit you'll be riding along with me to the doctor's office. We need your physicals as well as your heart and liver tests, and then tonight we'll be smoking DMT." DMT? (N,N-dimethyltryptamine – a psychedelic drug.) I'm here to get off of drugs, not for candy-flipping. I pondered all of this.

I knew what DMT was. A couple of years earlier I had visited my little brother, Nathan. And, at the time, he was a washed-up Dallas rave DJ, who had been in and around the electronic dance scene from the 1990s to well into the 2000s. Nathan wasn't washed up because he was no longer in demand. Nathan was forced into his retirement, but we're getting to that.

Nathan frequented the legendary Dallas discotheque, the Starck Club, in the 90s. Many people credit the Starck Club with the birthing of the Rave dance scene, as well as the drug, ecstasy. From what I know about the Starck, it could be considered the *Studio 54* of Dallas back in the day.

Joey loved to visit Nathan in Dallas. Normally an introvert, ecstasy brought out Joey's extrovert side. Joey would always return from Dallas a changed man for several months after, but he would clam back up little-by-little until going again. After such trips, Joey would tell grand stories about celebrities with whom he and Nathan had mindlessly danced and partied until dawn.

In one of the more memorable stories Joey always told, he had brought a pan of his "world famous pot brownies" to share with their crew at the Starck Club. The brownies later evolved into what Joey coined *"The Wookie"* as a fusion of weed and cookie.

Being heavily entrenched in the scene, Nathan always got Joey, and himself, past the velvet ropes and into the VIP area with all of the celebrities who were sure to visit the Starck while passing through Dallas in the 90s. Joey shared his world famous brownies with Dennis Rodman that night (allegedly), and if I heard that story once, I must have heard it a thousand times, but I never tired of it.

Nathan and I both found our way into an amazing existence despite long odds, but Joey had always depended on Nathan and me for his vicarious outings. (Still, many times, I wonder if Dennis remembers Joey and his famous pot bakings.)

My brother Joey had suffered more long-term psychological trauma from our childhood than Nathan and me and that was certainly exacerbated by Joey's tackle-box full of prescription drugs. I always marveled about that phenomenon. Joey took all of those prescription drugs, which made him disappear further and further into his own world, but just one ecstatic trip to Dallas where he would dance all night somehow made him seem normal and happy for months to come.

The annals of time have long since caved in on Joey, an amazing revolution, and my little brother's career and freedom, which were all squashed by the DEA (Drug Enforcement Administration) in favor for highly addictive chemical substitutes to MDMA (3,4-methylenedioxy-methamphetamine or Ecstasy) for legally treating disorders. I have never seen either of my brothers as happy as they were during those times.

Due to our tumultuous childhood, combined with their artistic eccentricities, it is not surprising that Nathan and Joey felt comfortable in that chaotic environment; I completely got it. Not long after Joey died, like Gramps, Nathan was on his way to prison. Nathan did some time, but, somehow, he narrowly escaped dying there. It broke my heart after mistakenly believing that the organ couldn't be reduced to pieces any smaller than Joey had already smashed it.

After that, Nathan moved to Arkansas, to lay low from the smuggling charge. That was the equivalent of putting Nathan in a cage. He often commented that he had felt at home in the city; that's what two years of camper-shaking will do to a person. Nathan often invited me to his crazy parties, and, looking back, I wish I would have gone with my brothers. It is one of my deepest regrets.

Nathan was arrested while driving a rental car with quite a lot of high-grade marijuana in its trunk. Nathan "had no idea how the drugs got in his trunk," which is A) why Nathan is still alive to *not* talk about it, and B) why I dare to discuss it here.

I was proud of Nathan. He had paid the fair price for what he had done and he walked away with a clear conscience. Though, what he had done didn't seem all that bad to me. Especially after what the legal tackle box had done to Joey. (President Obama recently publicly announced that tackle boxes such as Joey's had passed car accidents as the nation's leading cause of death.)

I can say with confidence that had Joey been legally allowed to smoke his pot and eat his *Wookies,* he never would have taken that tackle-box full of pills. Nineteen-thousand Americans a year now die from the equivalent of Joey's tackle-box—zero deaths can be linked credibly to eating *Wookies,* or any marijuana use for that matter.

Nathan had cleaned up his act and led a productive life as a law-abiding citizen. He was broken. Nathan had to all but ditch most of his longtime friends to change his ways, and he had MANY OF THEM. Nathan spent many lonely years after that, trifling through endless fines, jail time, classes, and nonsense.

Nathan was arrested in small-town Texas while driving the drugs from where my dad now lives in Dallas to Arkansas, where my mother had settled. If you know anything about the ignorant chemical laws in the great state of Texas, you know that is not good. Here is a quote taken from the *New York Times,* dated *April 12, 2014.* "We vote conservatively in Dallas, yet we love to break rules," said Wade Randolph Hampton, a onetime Starck regular who in the 1990s tried to produce a feature film about the club.

Having lived there, I know this to be true. When they say, "Everything is bigger in Texas," that is mostly true too, and, partying, as well as jail time for crimes that in Abraham Lincoln's famous words about prohibition, *"aren't crimes,"* is no exception.

At the time of Nathan's arrest, he donned an outdated fuchsia Armani suit that he had purchased at a second-hand store. He complemented the swanky suit with a man-blouse which peeked through the front of the jacket like a tuft of chest hair.

I'd also gathered from his mugshot that he had a freshly shorn facial hair experiment in which his mustache *became* his sideburns; there was no chin hair. Nathan might have had some Brian Bosworth lines shaved into the beard forming designs or something; I couldn't be entirely sure from his mugshot online.

Nathan was a flashy guy. Unlike me, Nathan gave zero fucks about what people thought about him. Nathan always just did what felt good to Nathan; he was a non-conformer. The rental car was a brand new Lincoln and the reason I knew all these details? Shortly after Nathan's arrest, he informed me that he had made the arrangements to "blend in."

Nathan couldn't quite understand why he'd been singled out by the police that day. Looked good on him, though.

One of the major elements of Nathan's case was a "mysterious powder" that the cops had discovered in a vitamin bottle, riding shotgun with Nathan. After much unnecessary jail time, the substance was determined to be my brother Joey's remains.

Joey's ashes had returned from the crematorium and Nathan had made the trip from Arkansas to Dallas to get his cut. We had divided Joey's ashes several ways to meet the needs of our sentimental tribe. Nathan may or may not have just figured that scoring a couple of extra bucks to pay for the gas was a good idea.

My brother Joey was riding shotgun with Nathan for his very last time, that day, when they took what little was left of Joey and stuck my other brother, Nathan, *in a cage.* One of my brothers was murdered and the other one was caged like an animal, and his career and his life were ruined, both for crimes that are "not crimes." And, I don't think those assholes ever returned Nathan's share of our brother's ashes after he was released.

(I launched my portion of Joey's ashes aboard a hobby rocket from the deck of the cabin that Joey was supposed to help Nathan and me finish building. The rocket exploded, high up in the atmosphere.) My mom was a sensationalist and she rarely called, unless there was bad news to celebrate. "Well, Tim, Nathan finally got famous," Mom said.

"That is great…. Mom, go on…."

"Yeah, your little brother did it, this time. He hit the Texas Top Ten." (I couldn't hear her sarcasm; I figured he'd gotten the record deal.)

"What's that, mom?"

"Well, Google it, Tim. It's the Top Ten most wanted criminals in the state, that's what it is. And Texas is a big state." (Mom would always add a little kick of production to any story worth telling in the first place. But this time, the story didn't need any additional flare.)

Nathan was a good kid. He was just doing what he had to do for survival, just like me. But we don't choose where we fit in. Nathan owes his Texas Top Ten infamy to a particular calamity in which Nathan escaped from jail. You heard right; he escaped from jail.

Nathan didn't tunnel out of jail like *El Chapo Guzman.* He didn't remove loose mortar between the blocks of his cell with an old spoon and make a paper mache head with his hair glued to it. Nathan didn't even grind through the steel bars with an old, dull hacksaw blade.   Nope, no sir, Nathan simply rope-a-doped those donut eaters and walked right out the front doors to freedom. That's how Nathan made it on the Texas Top Ten. Not because he killed a family with a camp hatchet or shot up a bank.

It all stemmed from some petty charges that Nathan didn't do and wasn't copping to. I didn't see little brother for nearly a decade after that episode.   That ended little brother's hopes of becoming an international DJ. Not because he was apprehended by the long arm of the law either.

Nope, no way. Nathan began a lucrative career of promoting dance parties instead. I'm sure a few of his beats survive and have been made and remade, but his hopes of fame were flushed down the toilet. Nathan has only spun records at the rarest of underground parties since then. Marques in lights with your name on them aren't good for business when you're on the run.

He just stuck other people's name to those marques and continued throwing dance parties that consisted of thousands of kids wilding out. I often marveled at the irony in that. Nathan was even interviewing and hiring off-duty Dallas cops to provide security for his parties during those years.

They never caught that slippery fucker. Nathan finally did the "right thing" and turned himself in after nearly a decade of zero contact with his family. Due to the embarrassment caused to law enforcement by the nature of little brother's crime, his treatment in jail was less than humane.

Making humanoids jump up and down till the sun came up was my brother's gift, not the business-suit program. He could hypnotize a crowd into his army of minions with the drop of his first beat; Nathan had become a God within his culture. (Anytime

I'm around Nathan, I make him bust out his high-fidelity dance gear.)

My family always thought of me as the straight-edge guy, and here I was the screw-up, and little brother was living a good clean life. No-one in the family knew about my problem, though. No one but Katie knew about my problem, and she was the only one in the world besides Dave who even knew that I had traveled to Mexico. And, those two still had no idea where, exactly, because "there" had apparently changed.

At any rate, while visiting with Nathan, in Arkansas, Brother busted out the DMT.

Admittedly, I was afraid of it at first but, after quite some negotiation, I enjoyed it a lot.

(Brother was also quite persuasive, in fact, he wouldn't take *no*, for an answer.)

Nathan still had that old, tube-style television set with a darkly stained, wooden console and chocolate-brown fabric covering the speakers. The cabinet had brass hardware. You know the ones. Up until about 15 years ago someone in your family probably had one, right? Nathan could have had any TV in the world – God, I loved that about him.

He dialed the TV to the "trippy music channel" and the ceiling of his house opened up as a T Rex swatted at me through the opening. The whole episode lasted roughly 25 minutes and that was a huge plus, being a hallucinogen. I had always said that DMT was the only psychedelic I would ever repeat for that reason. (I had experimented with hallucinogens as a youth but was in no way prepared to surrender to the mind in the twilight of my 30's.)

Wayne looked worried about the DMT activity too, which was scheduled to take place later on that night. Wayne explained to John, "I've never tried DMT before. I have, however, had a couple of bad trips in the past and I'm in no hurry to repeat that."

John reassured Wayne, "You have zero choice in the matter. The DMT is a prelude to the treatment and will indicate to the 'medical team' whether or not you can mentally handle Ibogaine."

What puzzled me, though, there was no *medical team* in sight. Again, the website had advertised an in-house MD along with a "psychologist, addiction-specialist, yoga instructor," etc, etc. That place was quite clearly not what they had posted. It baffled me that John didn't just level with Wayne and me, as to what was going on there.

John could have said, "Hey, fellas. I know this isn't exactly what we advertised, but you're here now, so, let's get clean. What do you say?"

I would have respected John for that; after all, I had started to feel a kinship with the man. But, every time I began to feel comfortable there, I would have to stop and wonder about why John continued with the apparent façade.

Wayne and I asked John questions like," Hey John, when is the *medical staff* getting here?"

At which time, John made excuses for every single one of the missing staff as if that were in any way plausible. The best excuse that John applied to most of the missing staffers was, "They're all stuck at the border."

The only staff we had seen thus far was Nurse Jessica. Wayne looked terrified; he just sat stunned when John finished.

Wayne's wife, Christi, re-entered the house to join us. John said, sharply, "Wayne, you and Tim are coming with me. We're going to the doctor."

The two girls chased along behind the group and begged, "Can we go too?"

Due to the chaotic scene as well as John's harsh segregation practices, I still hadn't caught either one of the girls' names. John replied to the girls, "FUCK-NO!! YOU CAN'T GO!! YOU TWO CAN'T KEEP YOUR MOUTHS SHUT!"

Wayne and I shrugged our shoulders at each other, behind John's back, while following John toward the door; we couldn't understand why the stress levels were so high around there. Also, it felt strange still having Christi (Wayne's wife) there tagging along. On our way to the car, John broke the good news to Christi. "Christi, I hate to say this but I'm afraid this is where you and Wayne will have to say goodbye."

I knew the look in Christi's eyes. I'd recently seen the exact "HELP ME" look in my wife's eyes. After a long, wet, salty embrace, the two released. Now crying, Christi sped north to the safety of San Diego.

John and his "new mental patients" loaded up and headed to a doctor in TJ who didn't appear to have anything to do with the Ibogaine University. We arrived at a small quiet "doctors' office" and went in. It was more like an alchemical lab with a simple front desk and a little señorita sitting behind it.

It reminded me of Gramps's secret lab, and that made me smile to myself. Old anatomical charts were hanging about and a skeleton dangled from a stainless steel frame in the small waiting room. The bones didn't appear to be plastic and the skull had a hole a bit larger than a .22 caliber bullet in the upper-left temple. Within minutes, the señorita called-me-out by name. After following her back, I sat down on an old gurney. Glassware and old relics of ancient medicine were everywhere. The walls were

Page 101

wood-paneled, and the place exuded the odors of a musty library with a leaky roof and rubbing alcohol. The same señorita who womanned the front desk had now begun pulling round, white adhesive styrofoam-probes, outfitted with silver snaps, from the backing.

The señorita asked that I remove my shirt and lay down as she strategically placed the probes to my chest, then watched a monitor as she drew some blood. The señorita printed some paperwork, ripped the page from an old dot-matrix printer, and hurried off. When she came back in, she began removing the probes from my chest.

As she stuck the probes back onto the original adhesive backing, I cracked a joke: "Are you gonna use my same probes on Wayne?" I chuckled.

She smiled and said, "No," while continuing until the probes all stuck-neatly back in their original places. I'm not sure if the girl even understood what I was saying. I dressed and went back to the waiting room.

When Wayne finished, he re-joined John and me in the waiting room. Wayne said, "I'm reasonably sure that she used Tim's recycled probes on me, during my physical."

"What gives you that crazy idea?" John asked defensively.

Smiling radiantly, I just sat there in anticipation.

"Because there were pubes on some of them and the backing for the adhesive was all wrinkled up," Wayne exclaimed.

We all laughed our asses off, all the way back to the house...fucking Mexico!

That moment was also when I'd began to take a shine to my treatment-buddy, Wayne; he was so cool. My hairs were on his heart probes and he still didn't give a shit. What a chill old surfer guy, I again pondered.

Wayne had a passion for Mexico as well as an appreciation for the resourcefulness of the Mexican people, and it must have been a result of the many surf trips there in the 1970s and 80s, I thought. The tales Wayne shared were unbelievable.

Due to my humble beginnings in that little camper, I shared Wayne's appreciation for Mexican resourcefulness. I remember the car ride back to the treatment house being an encompassing lesson in geography, language, culture, patience, and a great appreciation for Scottsdale. I was shaky and nervous due to my re-visitation of withdrawal, but the manic situation kept me alert. We drove back to IU (Ibogaine University), where we were re-joined at the kitchen table by the two girls. Tiffany (the blonde) began to whisper to Wayne and me. Leaning in closely, Tiffany said, "Hey, nothing is as it seems here; you will never believe this. Some crazy shit is going on—"

Tiffany abruptly fell silent as John walked in and interrupted her and I felt some fluttering in my stomach. Something was amiss, and, it seemed, these two knew each other far better than they had let on. (Ordinarily my keen sense of situation would have served me much better in that *setting*, but, again, I was kind of brain-scattered at that point.)

"What's wrong with you, John?" Tiffany, asked.

(Tiffany was quite the handful.) John again separated the girls from us; quickly sending them off on another arbitrary excursion.

The Spanish woman with the accent (European), whom I now knew as Isabelle, walked out of the house, exiting through the front door. Tiffany announced, "Wait up, Isabelle; I need my coat."

Tiffany dipped into a bedroom, which was directly off the living room. Tiffany zipped-up and ran to catch up with Isabelle. I began to whisper to Wayne, "Pssst, Wayne. Are we ever going to be assigned rooms?" John must have overheard our whisperings because he replied, "Well, when the crew finishes, you'll have your rooms, but for now, just leave your things right here on the floor."

I'd withdrawn $3000.00, in cash, before leaving Scottsdale, and it was in my bags, rubber-banded to my wallet. Also, among the contents of my bags, were an iPhone-5, which was useless at the time since I'd failed to notify my provider of the international-travel-plans, of course.

The bags also contained all of the credit and debit cards for every bank I had had at the time (including the business accounts). Additionally, my Driver's License, iPad, Macbook, and, of course, let's not forget the photocopied birth certificate, were all in there. I removed my wallet, but the cash and other valuables would have to remain there.

I was careful not to bring attention to my bags. I stowed the cash as an escape and bribery fund in the event things got out-of-hand, so it was imperative no one knew about the money. I was quickly learning, though, I didn't have enough drugs for the escape. It would have required brainpower for such an event and brainpower was something I did not at that time possess.

7.

Party Business

After the girls had left, as directed, John ushered Wayne and me into a tiny front room in which a short davenport rested against a wall. It was more of a worn-out love-seat. I had just watched a couple of nice Mexican fellas carry the flowery unit down the hall, only minutes before our summoning.

A younger fellow with a youthful Boston accent who couldn't have been more than 20 years old, sat cross-legged on the floor in front of us. Hayden had one of those hairdos in which the hair on top was long, but he had shaved it down the back and sides. Hayden had pulled his impressive locks back and tied them into a long, black ponytail.

I suppose one might have considered it a *party business* hairdo – a reversal of the typical *business party* cut. You know, business in the front and party in the back (otherwise known as your garden-variety mullet). Hayden's *party business* hairdo seemed quite fitting since the place also appeared to fit the same description.

Hayden wore a pair of oversized, round, mirrored sunglasses with peace-sign-shaped lenses, dangling from his shirt pocket by a single temple. Clown, I thought to myself. Hayden graced us with a lengthy review of some anonymous addiction program with which he had associated himself, during which, he explained his "higher power" to be the drug DMT. Hayden spoke, "Now, I'll be speaking with the two of you, concerning the psychedelic treatment itself."

(Earlier Hayden had been introduced as an "addiction counselor." Wayne must have had a chance to think about that because he raised his hand to speak.) Scrutinizing the possibility of any professional background, Wayne interrupted Hayden, "Quite frankly, it's just a matter of math, Hayden. Being an 'addiction counselor' isn't merely a pair of words, son. Do you know that, Hayden? It requires a master's degree," Wayne nurtured.

To which Hayden proudly declared, "I'm a surviving heroin addict and an Ibogaine survivor."

Wayne was respectful to the kid, but, I felt he couldn't identify with him, nor could I. Wayne was just better at faking it. Nice enough kid, though. I'm sure the younger crowd followed him around like a goose. But my bunkmate, Wayne, and I were a little too seasoned for his bullshit. Old brown clipboards to which Hayden had attached a single, clean sheet of notebook paper, were handed to Wayne and me. Hayden now looked as if he were going to cry. (I almost felt sorry for the kid, but he picked a bad group on which to practice his control skills.) Hayden explained the following in a shaky, unstable voice. "Anyway, guys, Ibogaine is a subjective, psychedelic experience. You're going to analyze your innermost demons, and many people liken the experience to ten years of psychotherapy, in around 72 hours. But, it can be different for everyone."

He continued, "Some people experience the intense dream-like state, just as real as we speak now. Some won't experience or remember anything at all. Everyone's different, but you won't need the visual experience to enjoy the anti-addictive benefit from the alkaloid. It certainly helps, though it's not entirely necessary."

I wondered, if I would be one of the lucky "dreamers."

Hayden spoke again, "Don't be alarmed when you see the dead people, either. It's also common to carry-on a conversation with a dead relative or ancestor. Don't freak-out." (The stability in Hayden's voice was returning some.)

"You'll be in the experience for from one-and-a-half, up to, three full days. Now take-out your blank sheets of paper and write down the questions you would like the spirit of Iboga to answer for you." (Spirit of Iboga? I found this very hokey, to put it mildly. Brother Bob ruined things for voodoo vendors everywhere when it came to me. I wouldn't have ended up in that situation for any other fucking reason in the world.)

"We've found, that stating your intentions can be useful for setting-the-mood to your experience." (Like a twisted Christmas list; I thought to myself and smiled.)

The only two items I scribbled down:

A—Why do I have existential anxiety?

And B—Please help me get clean from these fucking pills, PLEASE!

Hayden gave me grief asking, "Those two items are the only things you need to change, Tim?"

"Yes, Hayden, that's all."

Wayne was busy jotting a lot of things down.

We heard Grady and John walking down the hall toward the small room that we had occupied. Grady said, "Hey, guys.

Page 107

Hey, I'm sorry about this, dudes, but, due to an oversight, one of you two will be sleeping on this love seat here. We only have one room available. I will leave it up to the two of you to decide."

It was reminiscent of crashing at a frat-house back in the nineties (back then, it might have been settled through fist-a-cuffs, though). I looked at Wayne; he looked at me, and we were both astonished.

My psychedelic pal may have been around 65, or so, years old. He wore a white goatee, had some facial scarring and a two-tone-Rolex with, a black face, and a worn out Jubilee band around his wrist. The Jubilee band was a size-too-big, so, I wondered, if it too had been inherited from his surgeon father. (Being a salesperson, these were the things I would always notice, clues to someone's buying potential. All bad habits, even at work, but, it was human nature to do so, and, to let some of it carry on to my personal life as well.)

I had noticed earlier that Wayne walked with a rickety gait, so, I'd considered being the "volunteer," but first all the years of negotiating would come in handy. "Grady, I came to Mexico, to get clean, but, I need to ask you a favor."

"Yeah?" a skeptical, Grady, inquired.

"I'm getting sick again, so I'd like another one of those...sixty-milligram Oxycontin, please? Also, I'd like two more for tonight, if you expect me actually to sleep on this small thing."

I shrugged my shoulders and raised my arms convincingly in the end while looking down at the davenport as if the act itself somehow demonstrated its miniature scale.

(Finding humor in the situation, I briefly closed-my-eyes, mentally excusing myself from the moment, so not to break-out-into laughter. I've used the trick a thousand times while closing deals in the states. It worked like a charm, if only you commit to the exercise. The nervous smile had gotten me into a lot of trouble over the years. But, I suspect that gaining control over it is to what I owed much of my success. I'm pretty sure the nervous smile was how I'd earned that first school paddling from Mrs. Montgomery too.)

Grady responded to my charade, "We're not here to get high; we're here to kick dope."

"Grady, I don't think you understand the amount of *dope* I was taking. Even with those three sixties, I only have a small window of time in which to fall asleep. John said I'd be *made comfortable,* and that's not what's happening here; I feel lied to, a lot. Grady, I'd sleep on this Saltillo floor for a week if it meant getting-clean." (I meant it.)

"My man," Grady identified. That marked the first time Grady had ever smiled or had even made eye-contact with me when he spoke to me. "Okay deal. Motherfucker! That's how I know Tim came here to get mother-fucking clean!" Grady said.

Grady seemed to have an edgy gangster-ere about him. The sleeping arrangements sucked, but, at least, the tiny room had a restroom attached to it, and, I had solidified my last couple doses of that poison. It was worrisome to me that Grady instantly formed a personality, the minute I implied something might be wrong there. At any rate, with the sleeping-arrangement debacle solved, the two fled the tiny room, and Hayden remained sitting on the floor. Hayden, picked up where he'd left off. "You two are doing DMT with John tonight, correct?"

"That's what John said," Wayne answered. (Wayne had become my ambassador to Hayden since our personality conflict had manifested itself.)

"The idea of Ibogaine treatment is to make you comfortable right up until the treatment, and that's where the miracle happens," Hayden finally finished.

Jessica popped in and out, offering comforting smiles throughout the first day; a smile never meant as much. Grady, the enforcer, popped back in to ask Hayden if he could, "Wrap it up, dude."

"Okay, guys. Tim, I need you to grab your bags and bring them back to your room with Carlo."

(Another Mexican gentleman entered the small room, and Grady continued where he'd left off.)

"Carlo here is gonna conduct a routine search of your bags, for any dope or other contraband."

Grady gave Carlo a couple of heavy back-swats. (I just assumed they were a form of affection.) Awe damn, I thought, all my cash and other valuables are in my bags. Also, I'd stashed a Suboxone strip in the business card pocket of my computer bag, and I certainly hoped that they wouldn't think that I had planned on taking it. Honestly, I didn't intend to take the Suboxone film, but when I had conducted my internet research back in the beautiful USA, I ran across a disturbing story.

A sick fella, such as myself, had decided upon using an illegal underground Ibogaine movement in New York City. The necessary business details had been looked after prior and the sick man rented a hotel room, after which the agent dosed the poor bastard. The man must have been given a God-dose of LSD because he tripped for eighteen hours while detoxing from heroin.

When finished tripping, he was so sick and exhausted that he scarcely had the energy for scoring yet another balloon of smack. The agent of said network was never-to-be-seen-again, and

Page 110

they said the same for the sick man's five-grand. That story alone is why I'd hidden the substrip in my bag.

If something were to have gone down, the 'Sub' would have prevented dope-sickness, for at least long enough for me to evacuate the country. I'd hoped to bring my bags back to the investigation room, alone. That way, I could have pulled the cash out first. But no! It seemed, they had seen that movie before, because Mr. Carlo followed, pace-for-pace.

Carlo was a pleasant looking Mexican-man with a strong-looking build and a short, clean-cut hairdo; he was about my age. Carlo was friendly and spoke the best English of any of the help (though it was weak). Carlo was dressed in blue scrubs and matching athletic shoes, and he had a stopwatch tethered around his neck. Carlo explained, in a primitive form of English, "Jessica's the day-nurse, and I'm the night nurse."

Jessica rushed into the room, hugged my neck, and said she was going home; I was sad to see her leave.

Jessica had again coiled the scarf around her neck, and the lingering of a fresh perfume dusting was definitely present. After this arrival, I quickly threw my arm in a bag, flashed the cash at Carlo for his bullshit audit, and stuck it into my pants pocket. It seemed my entire contingency plan was unraveling, thread-by-thread.

Yup! With latex-gloved hands, Carlo went through every pocket. He found contraband I didn't even know was in there—probably from past business trips. My accommodations were meager, but, I must admit that it felt good finally having my own domain. Though the night-time was nigh, there were still helpers and tradespeople milling about the property.

We took a short break, and eventually we all gathered in the common areas of the beach house. I spoke, "John, can I use your phone to call Katie?"

"No, I don't mind. Do you mind if I listen to your phone call, Tim?"

"Nah, that's fine. Can we do it, now?" I asked (John wasn't budging).

Reluctantly, John got up and walked me to the back patio. No sooner than it took me to dial the number, Katie answered, "Hi, honey."

"Hello, my love," I replied.

"Awe, you don't sound happy, honey," Katie said.

"I'm not all that excited right now, but I'll be fine, Katie."

"Why baby?" she asked.

I looked over at John who now stood nearly elbow-to-elbow with me.

"No reason, baby, I'm just ready to get on with-things, you know?"

(What I wanted to say was, "This seems like a horribly creepy trap, and I need to get out of here now.")

"So, you do the-Ibogaine-thing in the morning but what are you doing now?" Katie changed the subject. (Katie has always been a quick study; she seemed to know I couldn't speak freely.)

"Well, everyone's getting ready for a DMT session, in a bit."

I knew Katie would hate that. She didn't even like for her close friends to smoke pot. (That was like pulling the pin on a grenade, just a matter of seconds, now......) "What are you doing that for, Tim?" Katie asked. She always said my name when she felt agitated.

Page 112

"It's all part of the treatment, love," I added.

John displayed some quick-finger-motions toward his arm where a watch might usually have been.

"Well, I have to go, Kate, but I love you and the girls more than life itself; do you know this?" (Sometimes I just called her Kate.)

"Yes, I do, honey," Katie confirmed.

Normally, there would've been a two-day-heater had I mentioned a DMT session, but sensing the overall weight of the situation, Katie took the high-road. There followed a whole dialogue of sappy talk after which we cautiously said goodbye.

When others stepped out to smoke, I would usually join (I didn't smoke, anymore, really. I would just stand out there with them to keep my mind occupied). The view from the back patio was gorgeous. On one such occasion, Wayne and I were finally alone with the other girl patients who were giggly and Tiffany seemed kind of immature, at first. Unsolicited, Isabelle informed Wayne and me, "I'm an author from Spain, but I now live in Southern California."

Poor thing; Isabelle's husband had left her for a younger model.

"Were you hooked on drugs?" I asked.

"Oh no," Isabelle said. "I never used...a...droogs...in my whole life." Her accent was cute (the little English Isabelle spoke was proper just hard to understand). She was around 45 years old and wasn't an unattractive lady. Though seemingly naive, Isabelle didn't seem at all judgmental toward those of us who were drug-addicts.

"If not for drug-addiction, why are you here?" I asked Isabelle.

"No, no, no," again, Isabelle assured me. "I am here because my therapist ran out of treatments for my depression. She is the one who suggested the Ibogaine treatment."

"So, Ibogaine is the first drug you've ever tried?" I asked.

"Yup."

"Beastly," I added.

The same conversation exposed that she is—get this—a self-help author. The lady was a scattered mess of emotions, insecurities, and over-analyzations. It was apparent by Isabelle's actions too that she was proud of herself for having stepped out of her comfort-zone to take part in that bizarre countercultural-experience. I didn't know her, but I was also proud of her. Isabelle was a super sweet and genuine person and, thus far, she had claimed that the Ibogaine therapy had been an inordinate success. Isabelle bubbled over with excitement about the shit. It was strange. Almost like she was holding in an epic secret only because she had no way to tell it to me.

(Again, there were windows across the back of the house that overlooked the patio on which we stood.)

Isabelle pointed inside to the lighted kitchen table at a slim, paperback book. The ambiance inside was perfect; the light over the table cast a perfect flash of light over her new book. "That is the latest book I wrote, Tim, if you want to have a look sometime." Isabelle was so enthusiastic over even small things. I really couldn't wait to read her book, if I lived to read again, I thought.

I thanked her for her generosity, and the four of us realized our opportunity to talk, so I began. "Now, what have you two been trying to tell us since we've been here?" I asked.

I directed my query more toward Tiffany since Isabelle had the language barrier and efficiency was critical. Tiffany explained:

"I wasn't even treated here at Ibogaine University. I underwent treatment at Dr. Pollardo's clinic." (That was the first clinic I was supposed to attend.) Tiffany continued, "Pollardo was the biggest asshole I've ever been around."

"Why are you here, Tiffany?" I asked the tall, young blonde.

"Because I was on tons of Xanax, Tim, and, as you know, the Ibogaine does nothing for *Benzo* withdrawal. Now they're tapering my Xanax here. I was tossed-out of doctor Pollardo's jail because he kicked me out for bad behavior – fucking tool. My mom won't let me come home either, until I'm off of everything.

"She's a bitch too. I mean, I know she loves me, but, mom never had any time for me. She'd been over-absorbed with superficial bullshit. I thought my nanny was my mom until I was seven-years-old."

Now, I recognized Tiffany's physical pain because she had shaded her eyes with those swanky, large-lensed, white, plastic sunglasses. She also had a scarf wrapped around her head in a way that it had almost appeared to be a hood that neatly tied under her chin. The ocean-air pushed her uncovered hair, and it also gently moved the scarf's loose package in rhythm with its frequency. At that moment Tiffany looked unusually classy, like Jacqueline Kennedy-Onassis. I just assumed that her upper-class upbringing was shining through. Her attitude seemed confident too, considering she was detoxing from Xanax.

"From what substance did you detox at Dr. Pollardo's clinic?" I asked Tiffany.

"I was on heroin, Tim. I lived in Golden Gate Park, San Francisco, for a couple of years. Also, I followed the band Phish for quite a while. I was so fucked up.

"All I wanted to do was stop using heroin; I got off, too. I was only on Suboxone when my mom called Dr. Pollardo. He told Mom that Ibogaine wouldn't treat Suboxone withdrawal, so I would have to go back to the heroin for a few weeks before he could treat me. Fucking crazy, right?"

"Wait, Tiffany. The clinicians suggested that you go back on heroin before they could treat you? Suboxone is harder to get clean from than heroin?"

"Dude, you're fucking kidding me, right? Suboxone is the Devil's drug. Those evil motherfuckers throughout the medical industry hit the jackpot when they made Suboxone. Those doctors can say whatever they like, but there is nothing more difficult in the world to withdraw from than Suboxone. That has to be why they made it.

"Every junkie knows that all maintenance opiates, *such as Suboxone and Methadone*, are harder to kick than heroin. And, both are also deadly opiates, just like heroin. They call Suboxone an 'opioid antagonist' but it is just another fucking opioid that is ten times harder to walk away from."

Tiffany continued, "It's a business model. Suboxone keeps you coming back week after week to get your fix, and, it makes heroin look like trying a withdrawal from a candy cane habit. So, they never have to worry about you quitting again. Their Mercedes lease payments are safe."

And, she kept going, "That's how those fat fuckers drive those big flashy cars and wear those gaudy gold watches and shit; you know that, Tim. You live in Scottsdale. You see them jumping out of their Porsches with pubes billowing out from the V-neck of their scrubs and covering their fat arms. Who decided that it would be cool for doctors to wear their PJ's to work, anyway? It's sooo dumb!" (Tiffany laughed at herself hysterically.)

"Yeah, Tiffany, I suppose that you do have a point there."

I rubbed my chin a couple of times between my thumb and my pointer finger.

"I'd never had a rehab tell my mom to shoot me up with heroin before that either, Bro. And, trust me, I have been to more than my share of those shitholes.

"Here's how bad Mom wanted me clean: Mom was shooting me up with heroin in my neck, on the bathroom floor. I sobbed because she couldn't find a vein. I'd rolled every single vein in my body. Blood poured down my neck and chest. Blood was all over the bathroom floor, too. It was a murder scene. Serves her right for all of those years of neglect." More immature laughing followed.

"Your mom?"

"No, Tim, you don't get it. My mom is a goody-two-shoes, Orange County, rich-bitch who's never even pulled her own splinter and she's stabbing me in my fucking neck on the bathroom floor."

"Dear God!"

"That's not all, Tim. They took me to a hospital in Tijuana to put a shunt directly into my heart since they couldn't find a vein, either. The Emergency Room in TJ was so full of misery that they did my shunt procedure in a mop closet."

The look on Isabelle's face was precious. The poor lady had never even been exposed to second hand joint smoke before. But, again, she seemed proud of herself for taking part in that shit-show.

As the evening grew on, the beach-house emptied of the eager helpers and it took on a party-type atmosphere. I felt guilty about leaving Katie, to travel to another country, only to be cast in that sideshow of characters. But, you know what? Finally, it occurred to me that I was a well-qualified member of the *cast of characters.*

And, as insane as Tiffany's story was, mine was no better. We had different cultures and were from various parts of the world, but we were all there to take the most extreme measure imaginable to better ourselves. I vacillated between feeling excited about being part of such an incredible experience and feeling like a total dumb-ass. I was confused.

Grady and John joined the four of us on the concrete viewing-porch and we all fired-up cigarettes simultaneously.

It had grown completely dark outside and the wind picked up. I could see and hear Highway 1D (The Mexican-version of the PCH) from the patio. The screaming Doppler effect of open piped Harley-Davidson motorcycles hypnotized me as groups of them whizzed by the house. As the sound volume hit its threshold and changed, my head followed the shifting noise of the scooters like a dog after a bright-red rubber ball.

Fading out of the conversation, I looked around and wondered if weathered Bandidos would ride down the Baja coast through the chilly night. Every acknowledgment of beauty while in Mexico once again dissolved my sentiment with guilt.

I returned my attention to the group, right in time to witness Tiffany pulling down the front of her classic gray sweatpants, well below her puffy-vagina-crack. She was exposing a tattoo on her pubic area that was cleanly shorn to bare skin. Grady and John both looked on with pleasure. How could they not?

After we'd all had a gaping peek, even Isabelle, Grady told Tiffany to "pull them back up." But, I'm pretty sure that Tiffany's sweatpants were already pulled "up," when Grady shouted. Again, Isabelle too seemed to be soaking-in the naughty nature of the experience. By that time, Grady had relaxed and now joked around with the unlikely psychedelic soiree as well. It seemed Grady was on some substance himself since he had certainly cheered up from before. The conversation began to revolve around past psychedelic experiences. There were a couple of wild ones. Here is one, in particular, worth repeating: Tiffany was at *Bonnaroo* music festival and had several sheets of acid in her pocket. She was following the band, Phish, at the time. She and her hippie squad sold LSD, among other things, for funding the epic pilgrimage.

Tiffany had had three sheets of tab-acid in her front-pant-pocket and, while enjoying the festival, she had forgotten about them. Before long, it had begun to rain. Tiffany said, "The LSD ran off of the sheets and had absorbed into my skin. THREE SHEETS OF ACID HAD ABSORBED THROUGH MY LEG, TIM. My friends just left me there in the rain to fend-for-myself. Yeah, I've had a rough little go of it, and, to-top-it-all-off, I have Hepatitis C. Hep-C is pretty standard with IV drug users, and, at the time, the cure was ungodly expensive and not very well-known. Still is expensive.

"Golden Gate Park was fraught with smack, but, somehow, I was out of drugs and rigs one day. I saw an older, black, homeless man, banging-dope. I told him I'd suck his dick if he'd share with me and he obliged, so I quickly did the deed. I love to fuck," Tiffany unnecessarily added while beaming at the faces of the crowd.

"After, he only had the one needle that I'd watched him use, and that one he'd scored on the ground. Stupidly, I allowed the bum to draw water from a puddle when preparing the rig for me and I'm pretty sure that's when I contracted the disease."

That beautiful young girl had known evil in its purest form. It seemed like everyone had one or two great stories. The crowd appeared to be over the hype and after a brief moment of awkward silence, we all migrated back inside.

8.

Blast Off

"Hey, John, I need Timmy here for a minute before you get started on the DMT session. Do you mind?" (The two were more relaxed and I just figured they must have worked out their differences.) We entered the garage, which had been left open to the night where our moon cast its endless shadow over the highway.

Grady began to speak. "Timmy, I'm sorry if I came off abrasive when you...." (Grady paused to allow for a noisy craft to pass by on the freeway. The camper trip taught me to endear highway noise. I soaked it in and Grady continued.)

"...You have to understand, man, I've dealt with some of the shadiest grifters in the world, and I thought you were just trying to get high yourself. You chewed that second 60 milligram OC only two hours ago, and you're already sweating, *fool!* You weren't just trying to get high; I see that, right? We good, Timmy?" Grady finished.

(Mom used to call me "Timmy" – it always made me feel happy – I began to smile.)

"Yeah Grady, no worries," I assured him.

The two of us instinctually went in for the cool guy handshake. Starting with a loud palm-clap, with interlocked thumbs, we cocked our heads in juxtaposed positions and "pulled it in." Finally, we reached around for the one arm man-hug, and, after a few uncomfortable back-slaps, we pushed away and began to visit.

"What brought you here and what's your official title, Grady?"

"Well, like most, I was a pill junkie, Timmy. Starting out, I thought Vicodin was a fun thing to do when I was hung-over. It was dope. I'd pop a pill and feel fine. In fact, I felt awesome. I'd sit on the couch, nodding in-and-out while watching the little ants carry dead bees and shit down the little ant-highways on *Discovery*."

He continued, "Eventually, like everyone else, it completely consumed my entire life, and I'd usually end up on smack when things got that out-of-hand. I tried everything but couldn't stop the merry-go-round, so, I called Dr. Pollardo and filled out the online application. After reviewing my app, he called, and my weight and heart murmur tripped him out.

"But, I wasn't gonna to take "no" for an answer, so I ground his tits off for two weeks. At first, it was ten grand for the treatment. I raised it to fifteen-thousand. He still wouldn't bite. Finally, I got up to twenty-five-thousand-dollars and he went for it.

"We weren't gonna do shit his way, though. I wasn't gonna stay in his prison. We rented a private villa at a beachside resort in Ensenada and he treated me there. That's how I got the idea of just using a sick ass house instead of a clinic. A nurse watched me for several days, and I went back home clean."

"It was a miracle; I was insta-clean, fool. I thank God every day for that miracle. My wife, my little kids, and even my friends and employees said, 'I don't know what it is about you

Grady, but you look so alert and sparkly.' More than one person said I had 'kind eyes.' I was amazed at three things.

"First—I was shocked it even worked.

"Second—I couldn't believe I had paid that much. I'm a motherfucker, too, Timmy; no one gets me, *son!*

"Third—I couldn't understand why it was illegal in the US; I felt betrayed. Now I feel obligated to look after the people our government won't, Timmy. That's why I'm here."

Discussing some of the peculiar goings-on at the clinic probably would have been wise here, but there was no point; I was pot-committed. Grady's little pep-talk made me feel more comfortable, though, and he must have felt it also because he shared his Ibogaine experience with me. "You know how some people have the dreams, and some don't, Timmy? Well, I dreamed, and it was sick. Every time I shut my eyes I was looking through a different window in my head, and it was more real than you standing here now.

"I was a little boy and my TaTa (grandfather) was talking to me as I once again sat on his lap. He spoke to me in Spanish, and I touched his long beard. That shit was the bomb, kid. You're gonna be okay, Zigler. After tomorrow, we'll be brothers forever."

I'll never forget that. There was a secret fraternity, and if all the claims were true, I would be among them. Grady extinguished his cigarette on the garage floor with his foot, and I followed him back inside.

There were uneasy nerves at the prospect of doing DMT, a potent mind-altering compound. Even the weathered psychonaut will admit DMT is one of the most epic mind-altering substances on the planet. Dubbed *The Spirit Molecule* by author Rick Strassman, DMT can send you on a spiritual, life-changing journey in under 30 minutes, at which time you are perfectly lucid.

DMT is naturally occurring in the plant kingdom and the human body. Some claim the brain excretes DMT when you are born to kick start your existence, and at the time of death, to soften the moment you cease to be. Many believe the Spirit Molecule is responsible for the "bright light," and "out-of-body" phenomena reported as "near-death experiences."

Here goes nothing, I thought to myself as I made my way down the long hall toward the living room. All four of us "mental patients" were now sitting on the horseshoe-shaped couch which faced the brick hearth where John was perched. His tightly clasped legs prevented items from falling to the ground. One of the items John held carefully to his face while manipulating it with his busy hands.

It was apparent that John was no first-timer. Upon closer inspection, I realized that what he'd held in his hands was an empty, airplane-sized bottle of Hennessy whiskey. John pressed the bottom of the bottle to his lips. He then passed a couple of quick bursts of air through the apparatus to clear it of any debris. There was a hole punched in the bottom of the glass bottle to allow for the airflow. He then stuffed a small kitchen scrub-pad into the bottleneck. It had all the charm of any old homemade crack-pipe.

John loaded the glass pipe with a yellow bee pollen-like substance and passed it to me. We all sat attentively before him in a semicircle as if we were his disciples. I sat next to Tiffany on one side of the couch, and Wayne and Isabelle sat together on the other.

After handing me the pipe, John produced another from his lap, repeating the steps that he had applied to the first and handed it to Tiffany. So, yes, Tiffany was taking part in the DMT smoking-activities, although she had already been through the entire program (that was no ordinary drug-rehab). Somehow, as a group, it was decided that Tiffany and I would smoke together. John spoke. "There are only two rules.

"First, you will inhale until I say you're done, okay? No pussy-hits. Second, you may think you're going to die, and this is entirely normal, but you're not going to. TRUST ME."

At the same time, Tiffany and I put the crack pipes to our pursed lips and began to inhale a thick, cream-white smoke; it had a specific-chemical-taste that I would recognize again. When I had inhaled plenty, John noticed I had slowed my draw from the chamber.

"NOPE, NOPE, KEEP GOING," he commanded.

"You wanna get the full effect of the medicine. Right, NOW HOLD, HOLD, HOLD, HOLD, HOLD," John forcefully commanded. "Good, now, slow—ly...exhale for me."

It seemed John may have mistaken us for a kindergarten class. Tiffany didn't seem to need any coaching; she was a fucking pro. As I leaned back into the cold couch, I experienced profound euphoria. Bright lights and swirling colors forced my eyes shut; I could no longer see through them.

The colors had a physical presence, like a soul. For some, a profound spiritual experience can be had while on DMT but that wasn't the case for me. I had ingested so much of the powerful drug that it was a kaleidoscope of color and sound that didn't make much sense to me. Tiffany laughed strangely. Her low-pitched laugh changed pitch and frequency demonically. It seemed as if someone were telling her a story, and she giggled harder during the funnier parts. I thought Tiffany was looking and laughing at me; maybe that was it.

Maybe she laughed at my changing-expressions. But, with eyes open, nothing changed. I saw the same continuum of color and light. I couldn't see, so I remained with eyes closed while mentally trying to separate from the stimuli in the room. In the midst of the experience, I heard Wayne speak in a deep distorted voice in which he said, "Hey, John, if I..."

I sensed that John had stopped Wayne from interjecting so not to disturb my experience. Wayne's voice repeated, "Hey John, if I..."

Over-and-over, each-time softer than the first until Wayne's voice faded completely out – the colors still swirled. I heard Isabelle walking – every noise echoed. I again heard John say, "S-H-H-H-H, S-H-H-H-H, S-H-H-H-H, S-H-H-H-H" (but it didn't work).

Isabelle slammed a cabinet door when she arrived in the kitchen, and I heard a BAP, BAP, BAP, BAP. Afterward, I felt everyone's excitement-levels grow-considerably.

The DMT made me shaky, but at least my eyes worked again and here's what I saw: Tiffany held and rubbed herself all over with her eyes closed because she was fully tripping. Isabelle gyrated in her seat like she desperately needed to pee while laughing like a jackal at all of us. John crept on Tiffany; the look on Wayne's face was that of panic because he was scared shitless.

"Do I have to do this?" Wayne asked John.

John said, "Uh, yeah," while holding his laughter so not to embarrass Wayne.

John's eyes were still solidly fixed on Tiffany, but I must say in his defense, it was a lot for a young man to behold.

John was a brilliant psychedelic-sitter. He was in tune with needs and feelings, was articulate, and his voice was calm. Trying to enjoy things for what they were now, I began to think: I'd paid for the trip, there were supposed to be medical professionals, monitoring of vitals, and, as it turned out, John, was an expert tour guide. (That is—if—the "medical professionals" kept the appointment.)

John loaded Wayne's dose of DMT into the neck of the tiny whiskey-bottle as Wayne looked on with the excitement of a death-row-inmate being walked through the *Dance Hall* at *Sing Sing* Prison. But surprisingly, when Wayne got to the execution, he took it like a *G*.

He pressed the glass dick to his lips and sat up to take a deep pull. Though reluctant, this didn't appear to be Wayne's first party, either, because after committing he held the smoke forever. Wayne exhaled the plume and just sat there.

Wayne's expression went from focusing on something near to looking at something very distant in only a moment. Wayne's posture shifted toward earth, and his expression drooped. To explain the look on Wayne's face at the time, I'll use a scene from the 2001 *Spielberg* movie: *Artificial Intelligence.* It's the dinner scene in which *David*, the couple's *Mecha* (mechanical) son's face melts off after he eats the spinach.

Wayne came-to and was somewhat sluggish like he'd had a head trauma; he wasn't normal for quite-some-time. Remarkably, he didn't lie down throughout the entire experience, but, still John was more than a little concerned with Wayne's response. Isabelle, still filled with excitement, began sharing her DMT story until John denied her.

"You didn't even inhale, Isabelle."

"Yes, I did, and—"

John again abruptly interrupted her. "You didn't do what they did, so be quiet. Do it right now, then," John challenged.

"No way," Isabelle returned fire.

We all laughed. Wayne even mustered a grin through his fog. Isabelle enjoyed fitting in with the group of disabled drug-war-veterans. I think it made her feel...*edgy*.

Wayne pulled me aside to voice his concerns about our mutual choice of eating Ibogaine for breakfast the following morning; I had a flashback of jokes made to the neighbor about being "CEO of a giant B&B." I have to admit, now that I was staring down the barrel of eating that wood, normal rehab was seeming a lot more practical.

Wayne and I were both scared shitless, but, we each handled it a little differently. Wayne had no trouble overanalyzing things, and I mentally kept myself in the dark, usually saving the freak-out energy for the actual event. (The camper taught me to manage peace in the midst of the chaos, but when finally backed into a corner, I could still get pretty Old Western).

We all regrouped on the couch. John powered-up the big screen TV, then slid a DVD into the tray; everyone was in their pajamas and snuggled up in blankets. As the last person rushed in with a bowl of popcorn, the lights were dimmed, and Grady appeared quietly before me in the dark.

As the movie noisily began, the TV flashed brightly in my face while Grady handed me two more scrumptious brown Mexican-made Oxycontin tablets. A-H-H-H-H-H-H-H-H.... (Whew! Now we're talking. *I was beginning to feel very sketchy.*)

"A deal is a deal," Grady assured me as he turned his hand upside-down above mine, releasing the contents into my palm.

Page 128

If chewed, 120 milligrams of OXY was enough to enjoy what might be my very last Oxy buzz. Once-in-a-while I could still catch a buzz after a short dry spell; that's how the drug-addict thinks. I remember being envious, almost mad at the rest of the group, because they were all free from their vices.

Even though I was angry at the rest of the group just for being clean and sober, I was still worried about getting fucked up myself. The whole drug thing is a paradox. (Everyone there had only around a year of clean time from opiates except Isabelle and Wayne.)

The four of us watched the movie as John finished up some work matters on his laptop. Grady was missing, but John was always committed to his craft. On any given day, the guy buzzed in and out of the house answering yet more of those desperate phone calls.

John might've been walking out the door on his way to the gym and talking someone off of an actual ledge. His job didn't seem that bad. He appeared to do what he wanted to do and when he wanted to do it. John was haunted by that damned phone though.

I asked John, "Can I use the WiFi for a quick minute, please?" (I was desperate to talk to Katie.)

"I'm sorry, we don't have WiFi yet," John apologized.

It was annoying.

"I thought I'd FaceTime with Katie a bit; they advertised WiFi online."

"Sorry bro, we don't have it yet and I dunno what to tell ya, guy."

I was annoyed now. Go figure; I'm not passive aggressive, but somehow the strange circumstances seemed to have taken my voice. Maybe it was his personal WiFi or something, I don't know, but, John had been connected to the internet on *his* Mac the whole time.

Carlo, the night nurse, sat on one of the high-back bar stools that he'd placed against the back wall of the kitchen. The seat gave him a vantage point from which Carlo could see everything in the kitchen and dining rooms while also monitoring the hall. His elbow rested on a clipboard on the counter next to him. (He was mostly just busy taking his job seriously, I would have said had you asked me.)

Grady brought back street tacos from town. Though I wasn't terribly hungry, I forced myself to eat since I likely wouldn't be eating again for days. UGH! We stayed up somewhat late, but one-by-one everyone slipped off to bed, leaving Wayne and me alone in the living room. Visiting ensued. He expressed thanks for my volunteering for the front-room.

"Where are you staying, Wayne?" I asked.

"Come and see, dude."

Making quick work of the couple steps next to the hearth, I skipped into a grand master bedroom; I'd finally become very relaxed. Wayne's bedroom was on the back of the house, and it too opened up to the Pacific Ocean.

We walked onto Wayne's private concrete viewing patio, and I nearly lost my breath. Small yellow lights brightly peppered the Coronado Islands on a black backdrop. I looked to the left and then to the right as a giant moon shone just bright enough to illuminate the seventy-foot bluff from which we dangled.

A brightly lit channel of flickering swells gleaned earth's water in the moon's direction as it slightly pulled organic froth upon far away sands; I smelled the ocean breeze, which seemed to correspond to the sound of crashing waves.

"Wow, Wayne; good for you! What are those lights in the distance?" I asked as a micro-gust cut through our hair at once.

"That's a Mexican marine base on the Coronado Islands."

Wayne continued. "Funny story: There was a time when the US had a small Naval base over there on one of those islands, and I happened to be among those stationed there. I worked in the radio tower and loved those islands. The place is gorgeous.

"When on a solo-hump, one of my buddies noticed a white object in the scrub and identified it as the fuselage of a private airplane. It had some growth around it, but the plane seemed to be pretty modern. When approaching the aircraft, he noticed two clothed skeletons in the cockpit who scared him pretty bad.

"The soldier started back toward the base but after a few paces curiosity got the best of him. After prying the fuselage door open, he entered the wobbly plane, and, to his surprise, it was stuffed with rectangular bales. Producing his pocket knife, he slashed one of the bales, and a clean, shiny white powder poured out, dusting the floor.

"He dipped his middle finger into the white material, wiped it across the gums and, sure thing, his entire face began to go numb, almost immediately. He ran all the way back into the radio tower screaming: 'I CAN'T FEEL MY FACE.'

"We had more pure-cocaine than we could Hoover down. They're small islands, and there isn't much over there, so that was a treat.

"It was a small military base, too, and there weren't many of us stationed at that base, but everyone, even our C-O, was cool. We partied for months. But, it all went wrong in the end. We had some top brass visit, and they knew something was wrong straight-off. We were all a fucking mess by that time.

"The whole lot stayed entirely out of trouble in exchange for revealing the location of the plane; that changed everything. The brass got credit for our discovery, and we were all off the hook. My buddy, Bill, had what amounted to a couple of ounces stashed still. We only partied in TJ from then on though. That was our rule."

Wayne went on, "How no one knew the plane had crashed up there is beyond me. Little known fact: A pier built boardwalk casino was built just above the water on one of those islands during prohibition days. They've demolished it since and that is disheartening since the place was so fucking cool. Capone hung out there, and it was the Las Vegas, New Orleans, or Havana, of the thirties," Wayne finished.

With that, we re-entered Wayne's giant master bathroom, and there were mirrors everywhere. Noticing a full walk-in shower, as well as a jacuzzi-style tub with even more mirrors on it, I pictured a Mexican cartel boss relaxing there. My pills were kicking in pretty decently, so I'd decided to get to bed.

"Well, I think I'm gonna try and hit the rack, Wayne."

"Goodnight, Timbo," Wayne wished.

"Big day tomorrow, right?" Wayne added rhetorically.

"Oh yeah, I haven't forgotten about it, Wayne."

Nervous laughter ensued as I walked toward the living and dining rooms.

As I passed the dining room, I bid Carlo goodnight. He was still sitting on his chair keeping watch over the household. His head was bowed while he texted someone. He held in his hands an old clamshell-style cellular phone that he had plugged into the wall for charging. Carlo looked up at me with a squinting-nod, and his face was lighted blue from the glowing phone screen; he promptly returned to his business.

When I arrived at the small room I'd been assigned, I took a minute to assess what had just occurred. Oh my God...I'd hardly spoken with Katie, and, frequently, Katie and I were together during the week since I worked the weekday job from home. We spent our weekends together as well since Katie sold auto-insurance at the dealership; she was a broker.

We had been together for eleven years and had gotten along amazingly; I began to miss her terribly. I can remember feeling the constant burden of guilt for having put-her-through that whole ordeal. I walked back out to the kitchen and asked to use Carlo's cellphone.

"I'd have to ask Mr. John, and he is asleeping," Carlo said.

"Okay, never mind, Carlo, thank you."

I returned to the room and curled up on that undersized love-seat. It was quite hard, but I was exhausted.

9.

Our Mother

Sleep came, but I was up only two hours later, drenched in sweat. The scheduled morning plans were only part of the problem because waking up scared had become somewhat routine for me. Noisily turning on the lights and TV during a "freak out session" would ensure Katie's company and she'd rub me back to sleep or something nice like that. After years of the strange behavior, Katie finally voiced her concern. "That's crazy. What do you think about when that happens?"

"You don't even wanna know, Katie."

"Come on," Katie pleaded.

Sharing the source of my anxiety with Katie was a risky move, due to the subject matter, but she had asked, and it did feel good to talk about, so I said, "Fine, there's a lot of different stuff, Katie, but look... Sometimes I wonder what all this is for?"

"Oh my God. Are you kidding me?"

"Yeah, if we all just die in the end, or any old day, I suppose, then why should we even bother learning? Why bother learning to play the guitar better or to develop a talent, or anything at all, if we all just go away tomorrow? Think of the talent that's

GONE, like Elvis or Kurt and they barely even got to enjoy what they had, you know?" I paused.

"Everyone is going to die on a certain date. If everyone's gonna die on a firm date, then we're all gonna die in a precise order. And, the next thought is: In what sequence are we all going to die? That's all gonna happen, one hundred percent. Sometimes life just seems like one long funeral procession," I finished.

"Oh my God, Tim! That's absolutely awful," Katie responded.

That night, I anxiously rubbed Katie to sleep, and she'd never had anxiety in her life. (We've shared the disorder since.) Every several nights from then on one would "freak-out" while the other comforted. All manner of lies were then told until the victim fell asleep. It might have been a coincidence, but I felt horrible for my complicity in Katie's new disorder.

I sprang from the davenport. (Let's take a small time out here: Imagine having to go through detox in a strange country. Now imagine staring down the barrel of a "72-hour trip on a drug boasting a 1/300 death rate," WHILE DETOXING.)

Really, Tim? The *Tim* who booked this appointment sure didn't care about the *TJ* Tim. Fuck that Tim, I thought. But I knew, today Timmy was the lucky boy who would pay for the monumental misstep. Today Timmy gets to eat African root bark for breakfast, puke his brains out, and meet satan after fighting with a giant demon.

Wait, I mean, over the next..TWO TO THREE DAYS! Oh my God, I almost forgot, I get to see DEAD PEOPLE too. It's all okay, though, because, at least, they would be MY dead relatives. For the benefit of the organism as a whole, I would have to take one for the team but FUCK ME, I thought. FUCK ME. While pacing the floor of the little room, I had a whole conversation with myself.

OH FUCK, I thought. Crashing through the door of the tight chamber, I limped down the hall, and a statue of Mother Mary stopped me in my tracks.

Our Mother stood inside an arched, lighted recess in the orangish-brick hallway wall. Cloaked and hooded in blue, she looked at my feet. I, for the first time, realized why Mary renderings look to the ground: If our mother had been looking me in my eyes, the shame alone might have killed me in my socks.

My earth mother had recently converted to Catholicism. I thought it rounded out her respectful grouping of ex-cults and religions handsomely, but Mom seemed happy. I remember thinking, maybe it's a funny way of slowing down in her old age – out with the charismatic, evangelistic churches with young dude rock bands and in with holy water and wine.

Funny thing: Mom didn't drink alcohol until she was Catholic and now she had made wine with fruit grown herself. Mom had only recently converted to Catholicism, so I took the statue as a sign that I would be okay. This statue was important, even though there was a Catholic shrine every several kilometers in Mexico as well as in almost every home.

I was in a strange place physically and emotionally, and I couldn't get my anxiety under control. My phone didn't work there, and I felt lonely because everyone was asleep, and I didn't even have a bedroom.

I turned away from the statue, whose pose I had suddenly assumed, and there stood Carlo. I folded my arms and Carlo placed his hands on my elbows.

"Are you okay? Why you yell?" Carlo asked.

I suddenly realized that the conversation in my quarters with myself wasn't "with myself."

"I'm so scared, Carlo, I think I'm losing my mind… Oh my God – oh my God, Carlo."

"You be okay, follow me," Carlo said.

Carlo led me down the hall to the living room, and though dark, I could see that Carlo had fully extended the recliner on his side of the couch.

"Pulling, uh the thing uuuuuuuhaeir, okaeey?" Carlo groaned.

After taking a seat, Carlo enjoyed a celebratory toe wiggling beneath the blanket with which he'd covered himself.

Carlo hand-gestured hintingly at a matching recliner handle, hiding on the other side of the couch, which I easily found. I was still beyond scared but found some comfort in being with Carlo. Carlo and I couldn't speak very efficiently but seemed to understand each other fine. I felt my body relaxing, so I snuck past Carlo toward my assigned room and from the microwave clock I noticed it was 4:00 am. After curling up on the tiny davenport, I prayed myself back to sleep but again awoke with a jolt. My body was worked and withdrawal came early, but I was thankful for the couple hours of sleep.

WOW! I was more comfortable and ready for the experience than I had been the previous night —THANK GOD. The waiting itself was the worst of it. My body was contorted, sore, and stiff but I walked out of the room anyhow. The fog inhibited my view of the ocean from the dining room windows. (The place was no longer the party it had been but, was soon to be a *party* of some sort.)

I went outside and poured myself into the hammock. (Staying busy until the doctor arrived was important. There were times when panic caused early acute withdrawal. I had learned to manage the symptoms; I had worked through lean times before. Hell, there were times when there wasn't a pharmacist in Phoenix who could fill my script for days, when their business got real good.) The cold, sticky morning air kept me comfortable as long as I rocked with my leg. Swinging the hammock reduced anxiety; lack of the painkiller's sedating effects had caused what some call restless legs syndrome, which in my experience can lead to body tremors. Katie called it, "Jumpy legs." While rocking for hours in the swing, I pondered the planned event.

Wayne was still sleeping, so I walked back into the beach house leaving the heavy sliding door open. When back inside, I noticed Carlo was nowhere to be seen and the blanket he used was folded neatly to the side. The doctor was supposed to be there by 8:00, so I shouldn't have to wait long, and it must be almost 8:00 now, I estimated. How does a whole houseful of adults sleep past 8:00? I was again puzzled.

Suddenly the door cracked open, and five Mexican workers poured through it. The door closed-promptly behind them, and they were each off on their separate missions.

One walked toward the garage and when the interior garage door shut, I heard a washing machine-hatch slam. The short, skinny guy with the pencil mustache who wore checkered chef pants unloaded a brown-paper sack full of groceries; he wasted no time rattling the cooking implements against pots and pans while the rest scattered to unknown regions. Typically, the racket would have driven me nuts before my morning meds, but I was glad to have people around, so I relished their angst.

Because we have a large population of Spanish speakers in Arizona, I only spoke enough Spanish to get what I needed in almost any situation. It was mainly at work that I would get to use some broken Spanish, but I didn't speak much.

"Comida?" Chef asked.

"Soy poquito inferma," I replied. (That means: "I'm a little sick"...I think.) Chef threw his long, skinny, pointer finger in the air and quickly assembled a grouping of items that included fruit and yogurt. Afterward, he grabbed the blender pitcher and slammed it on the counter next to the groceries.

"Si, si, a smoothie," I said.

(That sounded great.)

Carlo raised his voice to Chef (in Spanish) after sneaking up from behind us. Chef bobbed his head up-and-down with a quickness and returned the delicious ingredients. (Mostly, my Spanish was limited by time, just because they talk so damned fast, you know. If they wrote it down or spoke slowly, I could usually wrap my mind around what they were saying. That's why there's longer dialogue with some of the non-English speakers; we had time to work it out. Carlo was scolding Chef for making me a smoothie when we left off.) "You can't have those," Carlo said.

Carlo slowly removed a pair of fake "Ray-Ban Aviators" from his eyes and placed them on the counter along with a set of rental car keys. (Both lenses boasting—"Ray Ban"—instantly gave them away.) I sat in front of Chef's station, attempting to kill some time while watching him work. Not being electronically connected to the world was foreign to me, and it would've been relaxing there had I felt normal.

It was almost 9:00 AM, and I was far-too-sick and exhausted for being nervous about the treatment; now I just wanted relief of any kind. Annoyed, I moved back to the couch in the living room. At about that time, Grady appeared to be walking down the hall toward me.

"Whatsup guy? Are you ready for your big day?" Grady asked.

"It seems I'm the only person ready for my 'big day,' Grady."

"Awe, C'mon, Timmy. I can see you're getting sick, bro. The Dr. called, and he's running a little late. He's having trouble getting through the border."

(That was everyone's convenient excuse except when they finally got through the border, they all appeared to be 100% Mexican.)

Grady took a seat next to me on the couch.

"Fuck me, Grady, really," I whined.

"You're gonna be fine Timmy. Watch; on this beautiful beach day, you get YOU back, bro. Get excited, fool. Then, when you're all done, we're gonna show you how to enjoy a clean life because there's tons of cool shit to do around here."

(Might it really be the day I'd...."get me back?" The idea alone lent me a sharp sense of bravery. Might that have been my last evil tablet? I wondered. Also, I had detoxed enough to know that there was going to be no fun had for months, but Grady certainly sounded convincing. I just assumed that everyone sugar-coated the events following treatment.) Grady had a way of making me feel like I was one of the "homies," though I clearly wasn't.

Chef walked in and subserviently handed Grady a bowl of cereal. He eye-fucked the offering as he smacked his lips. His fro was all fucked up from a good night's sleep, and he was still in the clothes he'd slept in the night prior. Grady wore black

Page 141

basketball shorts which looked long, really long, and a faded black t-shirt bearing holes of various sizes.

Grady began making small talk. "To be fair, Timmy, I gave you my story last night so what's yours?"

Offering the usual rundown, I gave him the whole two-job-bit and explained how I'd gotten caught in the opiate trap.

"Wow, bro, that's pretty serious shit," Grady replied between lip-smackings.

(It sounded like an auto-response since Grady mostly occupied himself with molesting the oatmeal Chef had handed him. He was nearly halfway through it, and had already displayed some promising new eating moves; I grew up in a house full of growing boys too.)

"What's your background, Grady?"

"Well, Timmy, I'm 'Dog the Bounty Hunter' of Dallas. I'm really just a bail bondsman, but that's the business I'm in. I have several locations around the Dallas area."

"At some point, you might've bonded my little bro, Grady. He also lived in Dallas forever and got into his fair share of trouble."

"What's his name, dude?"

"His name is Nathan, and he's one cool guy," I told Grady of my brother's smuggling charges and how he'd been in Arkansas after losing a load, etcetera. "Nathan was dealing with the mafia, Grady. They're some bad dudes. My older brother OD'd in Nathan's house when Joey was living with Nathan. Some of the stories Joey told about Nathan kept me awake at night."

"Hmmm," Grady grunted.

"Here is one I can talk about Grady. Yeah, he was charged with 'Engagement in Organized Criminal Activity,' or something

Page 142

like that. Some kid had swiped Nathan's money while riding shotgun beside Nathan (the cash was in Nathan's console). Nathan had
no idea who'd stolen his money at first, since the car was full of
people. 'If we're all friends here, and we all trust each other, then
everyone empty your pockets,' Nathan threatened the passengers."

Nathan's car was full of people.

"The kid leaped out of the car and made off running.
Nathan gave chase, close-lined the kid from behind, and gave him
a subtle beat down. Nathan's friends then proceeded to kick the
shit out of the kid, Joe Pesci-style. The report stated: 'Nathan was
still attempting to pull his gang from the boy when we got there.
The victim mumbled about shitting his pants, or something, then
fell asleep.' The kid didn't wake up for six weeks after that."

"You're DEA," Grady interrupted, as he turned toward me
slowly. [DEA = Drug Enforcement Administration.]

"WHAT THE FUCK ARE YOU TALKING ABOUT
GRADY?" I asked.

I couldn't believe what I was hearing? I looked back down
in contemplation.

"What makes you say some shit like that, Grady?"

"It's obvious by the way you speak and the way you carry
yourself bro; you talk like a cop, Tim. I would know. "

(By this time, I'd wrapped myself in Carlo's blue blanket,
head-bowed, eyes-closed, and again, shivering.)

"Grady, that doesn't make any sense, man? What would
DEA be doing in a legal, Mexican establishment?"

I rotated toward Grady with a pleading look on my face
and to my dismay, he was already fast asleep. Grady endlessly
snored while sitting upright. He started out strong, but thundered

as time passed. The helpers too made the sound of a charging-cavalry.

Time dragged by as the Mexican beach house slowly came alive. Grady's Goliath head flopped back, after being repelled by a sudden exhale, a delay, then a sudden inhale propelled it back into its bowed position. His head continued its awkward orbit—back, front, and side-to-side, as the giant head flopped around. At first I was concerned, but not to worry as the rolls on Grady's thick neck caught the giant gourd like a trusty neck-brace. His cheeks flapped violently, and I grew iller with every random occurrence. Just when I thought I couldn't be any more miserable, John walked in (well, Hallelujah).

"Are you okay, Timbo?" John inquired.

"No, dude," sweat tears and snot-drenched the collar of my blanket.

I laid on the couch completely horizontally next to Grady, and he was still snoring. A failed attempt at rocking upright to view John had caused him to assure me that a "Dr. Silva will be arriving any minute." John pointed and laughed at Grady's snoring, and while doing so, I asked for more phone time. It was my last opportunity to speak with Katie before the circus was scheduled to begin.

John helped me to my feet with his left hand while thumb-dialing Katie with his right; he slowly limped me to the patio. We walked out through the sliding door that I had left open earlier, and his external iPhone speaker began to ring. John handed me the phone and headed back inside. He must have assumed he could hear everything from the living room since the door was stuck open.

The cold ocean breeze met my face, elevating my spirits enough to speak with Katie for a few minutes.

"Hi, Honey," Katie acknowledged in an artificially upbeat voice.

I tried responding but remember only blubbering.

"Oh, Honey. Are you okay?" Katie asked.

"No, the doctors are late, and I'm all fucked-up. They said, 'he'll be here any minute,' but I don't even know my name right now," I finished.

"I'm so proud of you," Katie said.

"Thaaaank you," I whined.

(Until that moment, I'd let on very little negativity about the trip, but now, I felt a strong obligation to accept some responsibility.) "Katie, I have something to tell you."

"Yes?" Katie asked.

"Nothing here has been what was advertised on the IU website. I'm a little nervous. I'm not sorry I came, but...just...nervous as hell."

(I was talking fast as hell too.)

"Oh God," Katie said.

(She and her sister both are over-reactors, but, again, it was all warranted.)

"John thinks he's Jesus Christ and has stigmata burns on his arm. I don't wanna alarm you, but I wanna try and explain where I'm at since neither of us knows."

I ran to the North side of the patio. "I'm looking at the Mexican Pacific Coast Highway, and across the highway there appears to be a school and...yes...it's a school. The sign reads: *El Colegio de La Frontera Norte*, right on the front wall. Oh...and it seems...oh...We're across from the Mexican Coronado Islands, or

Los Islas de La, *fuck-it*-I-dunno, whatever the hell Wayne said. It's a gated community, and we're at the northern-most yellow house in a line of eight of them—not all yellow, of course—on a bluff along the ocean."

"Tim, are you fucking kidding right now? I'm calling Dad. That's it."

Katie finally snapped.

"No-no-no, you can't. I have to follow through with this, Katie. Please don't tell anyone unless you have to."

She sniveled faintly.

"Thank you for respecting my wishes, Katie."

My heart did a somersault as John again rushed me off the phone. (I wondered if mercenaries would come crashing into the room while I was submerged in a multi-day psychedelic trip. Katie's dad was no joke. If he thought someone he loved was in trouble, he would get that person out of it, no matter the cost, rest assured.)

John said nothing as we both stared blankly at the Pacific Ocean. I think he felt sorry for me; John sensed my pain. As I stared at the ocean through watering eyes, I spoke silently with God: God, I'm scared, and I know you don't owe me anything because this is all my fault and I deserve this, but, I can't bear what's happening. So, please, please give me one small sign.

You could signal that I'm going to be okay, some way, I pleaded. A giant whale breached between where we stood and the Coronado Islands. We began to verbalize an "aww," followed by a smaller calf breaching in almost perfect succession that silenced our short, unexpected happy-song. (Maybe it was an incredible coincidence, but the timing of it almost made me lose my breath.)

Page 146

After emitting a combination laughing-shivering number, John placed an arm around me and steered us back inside.

"That's the first time I've ever seen that," John said.

John placed me on the couch, and I tucked my arms back inside Carlo's blue blanket that still cloaked my shoulders; the shivering vibrated my teeth savagely. When I again tried laying down on the sofa, my torso fell to my side, but my feet remained stuck to the floor; this is gonna be a good one, I thought to myself. (Remember the "blubbering hunk of shit," I mentioned at the airport, well *here's fucking Johnny.*)

Isabelle and Tiffany entered through the front door, and as girls typically do, ran over and assumed caring positions. Isabelle began rubbing my head and face that I had somehow smeared snot all over. (I had always been very insecure about my appearance, but the sheer sensory overload demanded I surrender the behavior.)

Isabelle took the seat next to me, and Tiffany ran to "fetch some tissue."

"Everything is okay now," Isabelle said with a "s-h-h-h— sh-h-h-h—sh-h-h-h," followed by chanting in her native tongue. Isabelle petted my head feverishly while squeegeeing fluids away from my eyes and nose. The shame left my body and an evil fear crept up in its place.

Tiffany returned and handed me a kleenex.

Isabelle jumped up and said, "I know what I'll do," and disappeared. She returned holding the slim paperback book that she must have grabbed from the table where it had rested the night before. Isabelle took her position next to me and while stroking my head with one hand, held her book open with the other.

"Picture the obstacle existing in front of you and then visualize yourself just floating over it in your mind," she read aloud while enjoying generous peek-breaks.

John walked back in. "WHAT THE FUCK ARE YOU DOING, Isabelle?" John yelled loudly.

"I am helping Tim."

"Get the fuck away from him, Isabelle. You don't even know what's happening to him. You have no idea."

(Isabelle had been helpful, but I was completely incapacitated; I couldn't begin forming the words to save Isabelle from John's lecture.)

The front door flew open so hard it whacked the wall. Several strong arms scooped me off the couch handily, carrying me horizontally as I kicked my legs. We hurriedly descended large, winding stone steps with matching stairwell walls upon which black iron sconces with slender, candle-lightbulbs dimly flickered.

10.

Phantasm

A single blinding light shone upon me like the suspect at a police interrogation. My eyes were slits. A soft voice asked me to put on a pair of eyeshades lying next to me on the bed. So I pulled the eyeshades near and considered putting them on as I was told. But fear reluctantly caused me to bunch them in my hand instead.

"Those will be your new best friend," John laughed.

Using my fingers as eye-covers, I peeked at the light, which emitted from an adjustable fixture. So, I politely begged John, "Please push the light toward the wall, away from my eyes."

As the light panned to the wall, John's face came into a dim focus. He stood before the bed and the glow of the bulb circled his head like a shiny halo in a religious painting.

The single light was dim, but I could see fine in the medium-sized windowless room. My mood was ominous, and it felt dark outside though I knew it to be a cloudless beach morning. The bed had no headboard and seemed to be a simple metal bed frame outfitted with only a box spring and mattress. There was a distressed nightstand and a flimsy garbage can in the otherwise empty room.

The nightstand had an old ECG resting on its top. The electrocardiogram was ancient, and its size and yellow shades of heat damage were clues as well as the giant black-and-green tube-style viewing monitor. [ECG = heart monitor]

"What happened?" I asked John.

"You were kind of crazy, Tim. I think you may have passed out."

"Wow, that's never happened. When do I take the Ibogaine?"

"You already took one capsule."

"How many more will I need, John?" I asked.

"Oh, we'll play it by ear, but it depends on how that dose affects you, Tim." John advanced to my side and asked, "Are you feeling better?"

"Um… Yeah, I guess. I am relaxed now. OH, WOW." (In fact, I felt perfectly normal. I hadn't used a single oxycodone pill that day, and I felt just fine.)

John excused himself and returned holding an MP3 player and a tangled knot of speakers and wires that played some funky, new-age music, having strange instruments and a relaxing beat. As John programmed the playlist, Jessica came in and began recording my vitals while smiling at me. She covered me with a plaid Mexican-style blanket, and I was shirtless which felt nice. It was colder down there than upstairs or wherever I was before.

I closed my eyes again. Maybe I was falling asleep. I was puzzled but almost instantly I felt the two slip out of the room and that squashed the tired feeling. (When the opiate routine is interrupted, typically there is no resting, so that was a good sign.)

As soon as John and Jessica left the room, I was wide-awake again. What was this going to be like, I wondered. As the time passed, the dim light in the room began to dance like a candle.

After a glance, the dancing stopped, only to return just a few minutes later.

I looked around and realized that there were closed doors on three of the four walls. There was one door in front of me and the others were on the walls to my sides. I wondered where they led. John and Jessica had been using the door to my left but as for the other two doors, I had no idea where they led.

I stared at the doorjamb before me, and a dinner-plate-sized spider web caught my attention for a second time, but a closer inspection left me to believe it had moved. It wasn't a web at all but a mechanical Daddy Long Legs spider. With deliberate robotic motion, the spider headed toward the ceiling along the left side of the jamb.

As I peered even closer, I noticed that it had self-replicated and a trail of robotic spiderlings walked up the doorjamb behind the mama spider. I closed my eyes and rubbed them with my fists. As I re-opened my eyes, I realized that the single object was again a static web.

"John," I yelled.   There was no answer. "Joooooooooooooooooooooohhnnn," I raised my voice some. Nothing... "A A A H—A A A A H—HELP—H-E-E-E-E-LP—HELP-ME," I screamed.

John ran into the room after several minutes of my theatrics and asked, "What, dude?"

A clean-cut gentleman wearing a white lab coat, jeans, and cowboy boots with those little silver tips on the points came trailing in behind John.

"I'm tripping, John. I don't know if I can do this John. This is crazy man. I haven't done anything like LSD in years. I don't think I can handle it John. I can't."

"This is Dr. Silva." I took a better look at the good doctor and he was a Mexican gentleman with bold-green eyes and a masculine jawline. He wore a fresh messy spiked-type hairdo, snug jeans, and a silk button-down shirt. He tucked the shirt into his designer-jeans, and a big shiny silver belt-buckle neatly cinched the tight package. Dr. Silva spoke fast. "Are you feeling anxious, Mr. Zigler?"

Though calm, Silva's version of the Mexican accent had a quick Southern-California flare. (It was clear that Silva thought he was the cat's ass with the ladies too.)

"No, I *am* anxious!" I shouted back.

"Do you feel as though you are freaking out, so-to-speak, Mr. Zigler?"

"YES," I replied.

(I was growing extremely frustrated.)

Dr. Silva stared at me for a moment condescendingly, then replied, "That simply isn't possible, Mr. Zigler."

"Do you feel like a giant, condescending asshole?" I mimicked the doctor.

He continued like I hadn't made the remark.

"The reason I mention that, Mr. Zigler, is the computer monitor here," Silva reported while pointing at the antique screen. "Right now your heart beats at a slow 38 beats-per-minute." (He wagged his finger at the screen a couple of times for dramatic effect.) "If, Mr. Zigler, your heart-rate is reduced from here, the alarm will sound and I will stimulate your heart using a compound, which I will be injecting into your emergency port. If your heart

Page 152

rate goes much below the current 38 BPM, that injection will be the only thing between Tim Zigler living and DYING. See? You are not anxious, at all. Your cardiovascular system is actually moving in slow-motion; it's all in your mind. Thirty-eight BPM, Tim," the doctor finished.

I raised my right arm and observed an ace bandage with a rubber dongle-thing dangling off to the side and my heart sank. I was in a panic, but my heart rate remained in the thirties, so apparently I had stepped into a mystical world.

The phantasmic Silva maintained his creepy, green eye-contact with me until a vision of him raising the stethoscope flashed through my mind. Lightning struck the silver object while the doctor laughed at the dark sky villainously; thunder clapped loudly in my mind. (I saw both events in sync as my conscious and subconscious met each other for the very first time. Oh, things were GOING TO get weird. I had wondered what this moment would look like but didn't imagine a young man wearing workout gear standing next to a doctor dressed like a vaquero on his way to a chicken-fight. A frat boy in his gym shorts standing next to a Mexican sorcerer doctor in a Tijuana basement. No, I never would have guessed that and that was the real part of the situation, so shame on me.

A bent reality came and went in waves and, as I caught another active fragment of clarity, I again observed how ridiculous the scene had turned.

Looking at John, I said, "I wouldn't do your job for all the money in the world; this is craziness."

John laughed approvingly. "Yeah, it is different, but that's what I love about Ibogaine, in particular. You are in a battle between good and evil and I get to help you win. You know? This part is a whole-lot-like an exorcism. We're exorcising your demons, so, I'm saving you, Tim. Psychedelics are incredible tools. You are now about to witness that first hand, my friend; they're so beautiful."

(I wasn't yet convinced of the Jesus routine at all, but, I could now see from where his power came.)

Reality had become more of a moving target, so I quickly sat up.

"How much of that shit did you guys give me?" I asked.

"Don't worry; we only gave you the test dose," Dr. Silva chirped-in. Silva wasn't near the sitter that John was.

"Test dose? That was a FUCKING TEST DOSE?" I growled.

Now and then, I would look up at the fellas who stared as if they were visiting the primate exhibit in the zoo. Thinking constant babble might dampen the strange factor, I verbalized every thought entering my mind. I rambled like a madman until erupting with laughter as I howled and dropped my head into my hands. Hysterically I laughed until an evil-feeling flushed my body and every hair stood on end, as I was scared silent again.

My jaw shivered as I clenched my teeth to an unsafe level and the taste of steel soaked my dry spongey-mouth. I lifted my head from my hands to see the men, and I swallowed nervously. Two witches covered with a white bed sheet were kneeling before the two men at the foot of the bed.

The outline of the witches' features was highly present in the bed sheet. Four creepy shadows danced satirically on the wall in front of me with the dim light's erratic jig. The weird music pounded away and seemed to grow in volume and intensity. I looked at John longingly. "Isn't someone going to be here with me, John?" I pathetically inquired.

"We have found that once things get rolling, it isn't good to have people in here with you. It leaves the patient feeling...a bit, uncomfortable. Many have reported mistaking the person in the room for a demon or a monster. Not good."

"John, I'm NOT okay, buddy," I said while ignoring the additional characters sharing the room with us.

I could tell John held back a grin until releasing a generous smile as if admiring the beginnings of an epic trip and it made me shutter.

"John, 36 hours, really?"

(John's smile grew.)

"Really?" I begged John.

"Dude, you're the one who's gonna see all the cool shit, not us. I wish I were you." John no longer held back his laughter.

"It's bad, John; don't you understand?"

The negotiation probably went on for at least an hour. I think John began to realize that your boy might be in trouble now.

The two men advised me to "let go," which was hard because I had such a tight grip on my monotonous life. Besides, the thought of surrendering to strangers in Tijuana for 72 hours, scared the crap out of me. (Are you kidding me? I was fighting to clutch onto every thread of reality I could for as long as I could, but nevertheless, "reality" slipped through my fingers.)

"Okay," John said, as he and Doc-Shiny-Nuts made eye-contact.

The doctor nodded approvingly at John, and John turned to me and continued, "If it's too much, buddy, we can shoot Alprazolam (Xanax) into your emergency port. Now, you won't get the visions that we consider so valuable to the experience. Be that as it may, it doesn't take away from the physical benefit of the treatment."

Then John stated, "Before you make up your mind, I want you to know that I opted for the Alprazolam, and I regret it to this day. During the past year, I've had to listen to the gains people have made. Honestly, I wish I wouldn't have pussied out myself, Tim." John finished and looked at the floor.

"Don't worry, Tim, I'll be right outside the door."

"Yeah, sure, John, you and Dr. Shiny-Nuts will be right outside my door, playing cards all night, and I'll be here in hell seeing the craziest shit I've ever seen."

"All right, buddy, let me splain some-theen to you," said Dr. Silva. "We will be playeen cards—[pause]—out there, whether you are seeyeen cracy-shit—[pause]—or not," Silva finished with a laugh.

(The accent had become a lot more Mexican and a lot less Californian.)

Silva looked to John for acceptance at the end while wearing a devious smile for the occasion.

"Well, that was *Tarantino*-esque of you to say, Doc. Cool, and dramatic. You guys forgot to mention bullying on your website."

Silva was making a joke of my condition and it baffled me. It had turned into bullying, but Silva was frustrated. The look on John's face showed his disdain towards Dr. Silva's behavior, and Silva was also denied a returned smile after the shady performance.

Silva was sick of my whining, but I was a professional negotiator, and so surely that got old quick. There was shrill laughter beneath the bed sheet under which the witches whipped jerkily like muppets.

Instantly appearing on the wall behind the crowd was a clean, white dry-erase board displaying a single blue word reading: *EGO*. The music elongated into a noise that sounded nothing like music until nearly shrinking back to the original song then stretching out again.

"Okay, Mr. Zigler, I will put it to you like this: You, are going through with treatment, whether you like it or not and there is nothing you can do about it. Must I remind you, Mr. Zigler, that you have surrendered all of your rights to us for one week?"

He continued, "You have consented to our treatment, in Mexico, and we would only need that paperwork if someone were to come looking for you. From this point forward, you are going to be clean whether you like it or not and what you choose to do with your life after that is on you."

With those final words from Dr. Silva, the room spun, and the music stretched into a native African-drumming, which grew faster-and-faster. At once, I heard thousands of bees spinning intensely around my head. (Once more, I saw from two points of view at the same time.) Mysterious winds blew the sheet as I watched the dim light dance at a terrific level. Still sitting upright, I saw the bees accelerate to the speed of a weed-whacker while circling my head. Doc raised his hand in the air and held it there for a moment as the evil in the room swirled all around him. Dr. Silva then quickly dropped his arm, and shouted the words, "JUST —LET—GO!"

At once the witches vanished, the bed sheet fell to the floor and the word ego on the whiteboard shattered. Broken blue letters gathered on the aluminum ledge of the whiteboard. When Silva

Page 157

spoke those three magic words, the last thing I remember is my body involuntarily flinging back toward the bed, and everything going dead silent.

11.

The Walls

My body fell through the bed-mattress in slow motion and carefully free-fell through the center of our Earth. When I had slipped through its end, I began falling faster, drifting further from our planet. Though traveling fast, eventually it seemed I was moving slowly since there was no other object with which to gauge my speed and no air pressure to disturb my clothes and hair once I was in outer space.

A rich collection of monk-like voices resonated in my skull, chanting "O-O-O-O-O-O-O-OO-OM," primarily in the chord of E. The noise shifted to that of a Didgeridoo, in the same key. It comforted me to the quick of my soul. Like zooming out from a waypoint on Earth, I floated further from the planet until the whole sphere came into focus.

With the greatest peace I've ever known, I viewed our Earth in total silence. (I traveled from a black mass in a dim, windowless room to the complete tranquility of our outer-space without moving an inch. The peace I felt while watching our mother, Earth, was powerful.) During the experience itself, time was not measurable; time became what Iboga made time become.

When Iboga granted the ability of zoom in on Earth, the population of our planet bunched up in crowds pointing and smiling while celebrating my existence.

Earth's many tribes were all present, dressed in cultural textiles while outstretching their arms toward me and waving as one great dynasty when I passed over the continents. Many of the tribes wore very primitive garb. This was mainly in Africa and South America, as well as the colder regions of the globe.

In many of the big cities in those regions, people were dressed just like you and me with business suits, trendy wear, and what not. The people in the great cities of North America were wearing the usual stylish gear as well, but many of them also wore clothes from many different periods of American history.

The African natives wore the whitest infectious smiles that made you want to be their friend or feel like you already were. All of the people laughed, applauded, and danced in honor of my cosmic presence.

Many of Earth's residents gathered around huts and shelters constructed from local finds, and, again, it was shocking how many primitive people there were. People who appeared to live in squalor and mud were erupting with excitement as I drifted over their continents.

Some of them lived on top of one another. There were so many of them; the whole world sent me off on a far-away multi-cosmic adventure.

Slowly, I orbited our Earth until over Tijuana again and this time I free-fell back toward the planet until crashing into the mattress from which I had begun. When opened, my eyes revealed the room in which I had started, but now it was dark; the single light had been switched off.

Nurse Jessica was sponging my face, which must have pulled me out of the vision. (I hate to call it a vision since it was one of the most real things I have ever experienced.) My state of relaxation defied the laws of medical science, and everything moved in slow-motion. I smiled at Jessica, and my eyelids were only cracks through which just a glow was visible.

The monitor's intense light was a comfort like the presence of a friend, and Jessica's smile was more precious than ever. "You see another world now; I can tell," Jessica whispered softly in the monitor's low light. I couldn't speak a word, but my eyes confirmed she was right; I felt incredible.

"What do you see, my sweet Timoteo?" Not only could I not speak, but I couldn't even physically form a sound.

Euphoria overwhelmed my senses causing me to squint my eyes completely shut. Long before I could speak, Mom called me, "Sunshine" because I smiled so much, and before then I had no recollection of those infantile moments. I only knew of them from my Mother's stories until then. The medicine was releasing some of the earliest memories of my existence.

Jessica pressed a bent corrugated straw to my lips and spoke the word *Gatorade*. With pursed lips, I took a couple of sour-swigs of what was NOT Gatorade, but it was refreshing all the same.

"Good, Timoteo," Jessica said, backing herself out of the room. "My sweet boy, what do you see?"

My eyes grew heavy, and I scanned the room. Being almost forced to close them – magically – I found myself in a post-apocalyptic New York City.

It was nighttime, and the place was destroyed. There was broken glass, cars were flipped, and so on. But, there were no other people in the city, just Mother, me and my four original siblings. (Joey was there too.) We were little kids and toddlers walking through Times Square behind Mom like little ducklings in the dark.

Every advertisement in Times Square was defaced, and every television destroyed. Sparks exploded from them at random. We walked as fast as we could, but we could never catch up with Mom. Then I was transported back to the room in TJ where black mesh had now covered everything. The furniture, the floor, the light and the walls were all covered with screen, and I wore a veil of mesh over my face.

Suddenly, a giant mechanical robot crashed in through the door, sending wall, ceiling and door debris flying. Titan looked like a giant, blue *Rock'em Sock'em robot*, with flashlights for eyes, that matched the stars which I could now see twinkling through the roof that he'd busted. Carefully I looked up at Titan's stoic gaze.

Titan grasped a black mesh bag full of data storage devices of all types, even ones I hadn't seen before. He was scary but still I felt relaxed. Titan turned his bag upside down and stomped around the room shaking thumb drives all about. The room quaked as he did so; Titan emptied the bag until the storage devices were armpit deep.

With only Titan's lighted eye contact, he outlined my task of uploading the data into my brain.

Many of the devices had embedded movies which Titan silently mandated I watch. The movies played in my head upon closing my eyes. (Make no mistake; when I call them "movies," because they *were* as real as anything in the world.)

Only after finishing my colossal task, could I rejoin the "real world." Titan tossed the empty bag in the pile and fled, the Earth again quaked as his giant feet pounded the ground. The black mesh covering everything vanished revealing sacred text upon those Tijuana basement walls. While sitting cross-legged on the pile of microchips, the print demanded my full attention. Black letters on bright, white-lighted background appeared as overhead projections on the four walls of the little room. The fonts were something like a dated newspaper, but the lines of the letters were all sharp and clean.

I read for lifetimes, and the projected cells automatically flipped when I finished reading them. As I read the text, my body spun clockwise 360 degrees and did so at break-neck speed, so I didn't have to move physically. (Once again, I saw from both vantage points; both from above and through my own eyes.)

I never grew bored of the content, and when my reading efficiency hit its threshold, deep voices hummed, "GUUUUUU-UM." Round I spun as text flashed on the wall, streaming volumes of data through my eyes and into my brain. (If one watched from above, that person would have seen me spinning around in circles while text flashed in my face like an all-night infomercial.) My intense reading continued until I took breaks for visiting other worlds and I enjoyed them best. The text was safe since it wasn't scary but the imagery could go either way; I could have an extraordinary vision or else my worst nightmare would unfold right in front of me. There were a lot of both; I never knew which until my eyes were closed.

Either way, the medicine eased the mental pain of the imagery. It did not, however, lessen the impact of it. It was mostly educational, and I knew it yet it was still very frightening. Disturbing my reading, Nurse Jessica held a small pleated white paper cup containing a giant pill.

"You have to take this Timoteo."

"What is it?"

"It is another Ibogaine, Mijo."

"Wow, I'm tripping balls and taking another one," I said confusedly.

"Good, Timoteo. Now you will have a nice dreams," Jessica willed.

Jessica again held the straw to my mouth. Finally she left and she passed John as she exited the room.

"John, can I to go to the bathroom?"

"That's the fun part, Tim."

"When you try and get up, you'll notice that you have severe ataxia. That's Greek for: you can't find your ass with both hands. Make sure you get help from Jessica or Carlo. Don't even try to go on your own, okay?"

"Fuck that shit, John! Are you kidding me?"

For the previous couple of years I had had a frequent urination problem, and so the restroom arrangements weren't going to fly with me. I'm not a fan of people "helping me to the bathroom" either. Rolling to the edge of the bed, I reached for the wastebasket and pulled it toward me.

"I'm just gonna piss over the side here, John."

"That's fine, Tim," John said laughingly.

(Stop now: I know it sounds gross but this was intense. I was completely paralyzed. Pissing in the wastebasket took a lot of stress off of the situation; so, don't judge.)

"I bet you've seen some crazy shit." *It was more of a statement than a question.*

John turned away and replied, "I have seen it all, Tim."

It took every smidgen of coordination to pee in that trashcan; the lonely light was off and that made it even more challenging. Other than extreme ataxia, I felt considerably sober with eyes open. The dreams had grown intense with eyes closed, so John made the following recommendation, "Open your eyes, and it will all just go away."

Only one problem, the "dreams" were so lucid that I didn't know they were shut in the first place. (Also noteworthy: I had astigmatism, which rendered everything blurry, but in my dreams I saw with clarity.)

My eyes were again forced shut, and I pictured myself as an infant; again my mother held and loved on me until the "film" sped-up. I then watched my whole life in fast-forward, reliving my formative years. I transformed into an old man, after which I decayed beneath the hard desert ground in a wooden box until nothing remained but dust and a thin piece of tooth enamel. After thousands of years, the shard of tooth enamel made its way to the top of a large mesa. The plateau overlooked a dramatic desert valley landscape and time slowed to real-time, human speed. The scene looked something like Monument Valley, Arizona. Katie's spiritual presence was sensed next to me on the tall mesa. My "shard of tooth" was partially balanced upon a pebble so when the wind whistled harder, the shard bobbled.

While pausing to admire the view, I noted that the desert colors looked brilliant. A radiant sunset appeared just above the highland in the distance. The intoxicating scent of fresh desert flowers lingered, and the glow of tiny specs of silica brilliantly flashed in the sun's light. Our ball of life dangled over its crop, flaming proudly, in its orange-silica haze. There was a profound sense of eternity as the sunset threatened the horizon, and the scene again faded to black.

I came-to lying inside a large, rectangular, cardboard box on its side in which a single light hung from the ceiling by a wire. The light generated heat like a ham lamp and gave the room a dim orange-red hue. The light shone on an object just below my feet that appeared to be a miniature UFO. The UFO was lying on a catering cart like the ones used for hotel room service and was the size of a large punch-bowl.

The ham lamp was positioned just above the UFO and warmed it until I smelled something burning. There I was in the hot cardboard box, huffing the burnt dog shit smell for days. Sweating profusely, I contemplated: How had I gotten here in the first place? As I reflected, the answer suddenly occurred to me. An old classified ad in my Arizona newspaper had lured me here. The ad had stated, "Addicted to opiates? We have the cure. UFO crash lands in Northern Mexico near Mexican-American border and will transform you back into a real human again."

Oh, that's how I got here, I gathered. (For the most part, the dream I was in at any given moment was my only reality.) Fear enveloped me. How could I have fallen for such a scam? I questioned myself. Drenched, I baked in the hot-box. One moment I would think: This is crazy, but maybe it's just crazy enough to work? With that, I heard teenagers walking around the box. They were laughing and shouting.

Now-and-then, the giddy groups pounded on the sides of the unstable cardboard box, leaving the ham lamp to shake violently. That would bring me back to my senses. Over and over again the taunting caused me to realize how stupid I was for having faith in that method of detox; nonetheless, I placed my confidence in the process.

For the next phase of the experience, that cardboard box was the room in which I would wake up. Because the "hot box" dream and my actual room in Mexico were so similar, my mind tricked me into believing that the newspaper ad was real, even with eyes open. Also, I think the overwhelming flood-dose caused me to lose complete track of our physical world at this point. Again too, that stretch of the experience seemed to take lifetimes to complete. I laid there in hot misery for hours, wondering what the youths' real intentions were, as I slipped in and out of more sinister dreams. My eyes again grew tired and were forced shut.

Alone now, I followed quickly, several paces behind Mother, through a dark and creepy forest, for most of the night. The nightscape was dreamt up by Edgar Allen Poe, complete with fast-moving clouds that whooshed passed the moon above dead, leafless trees. As I followed Mom up the cold, dark, and lonely trail, I could make out lights in the distance. Then Mom disappeared in the night.

As I approached the lights, I realized that they were windows in an old camper. Approaching the door of the camper, I again heard those unmistakable shrill-voices; they were the voices heard under the sheet earlier. Though I knew them as voices of evil, in the absence of any shelter or human progress, I was forced to knock on the tiny aluminum door.

The outlines of two haggard old women could be seen through the glazed window in the camper door. They were the same outlines I had seen earlier under the sheet. After slinging the camper door open, the witches introduced themselves as prostitutes in a supposed sexy manner. The two witches' sagging skin was covered sparsely with dated lingerie. They had feather boas kinked around their bodies and their arms were littered with track-marks. One of the witches was wearing dingy pink lingerie and the other was wearing grimy brown lingerie. They asked me to enter their filthy, stinky camper and being mortally cold; I wearily stepped in. With my first step, I fell into a small dark space and was tossed and tumbled inside the camper, back and forth, between two giant paint roller things. One of the paint rollers was pink and one was a dirty brown. The two rollers were spaced next to each other like a hand crank clothes ringer. Feathers, pieces of lingerie, two witches, and I were all tumbled about the camper like a giant washing machine. It was a frustrating and never-ending proposition.

A complex riddle would allow me to pass through the witches' camper, but I had no idea where to begin. It was daunting, and I can't recall what it said. Growing more disoriented with the magnitude of the riddle, and being exhausted from being thrown around, I finally blacked-out in confusion and exhaustion.

Now, I found myself as the feature character in an early eighties video game; I was the green block pixelated version of my myself. Most of the screen was a mass of channels in the ECG monitor screen, and there was clearance above my head and in front of me. It was like the video game *Dig-Dug* and I was in a small tunnel. Missing pixels formed a channel that trapped my video game superhero avatar.

Willing my computer-generated body in a forward motion caused my green figure to come into contact with the wall of pixels at the end of the small void. Instantly, upon contact with the end of the tunnel, my avatar moonwalked back to its original position.

After moving forward again, at the end of the void, I was forced via-moonwalk back to my original position. Mindlessly, I repeated the futile succession until painful. I willed myself forward until being pushed back, over and over as my sanity slowly vanished.

Iboga revealed a new scene to me: Lying there, I rested upon a now-smaller soiled mattress. The faint trickle of water dripped and echoed. One dim, oddly shaped *Edison* lightbulb in a metal cage shone from the now concrete ceiling. Looking down, I saw the shallow stream of water, rippling around the mattress, which appeared to be obstructing the flowing water. Human feces, plastic zip baggies, old syringes, Band-Aids, condoms, and all manner of other debris floated by with the stream's gentle movement. A peek over the other side of the mattress revealed my bags, which, along with my mattress, were soaked in sewer-water.

It was a rectangular-shaped, concrete-covered subsection of the Tijuana Canal. It was a scene borrowed from crossing the Mexican border the day before. Dirty human beings were walking through the water. The dirty people were shooting up drugs and having sex all around me. Just then the two dirty old women took the opportunity to snatch the straps of my bags. (I knew the two older women to be the witches who had followed me.)

A tug-of-war ensued, and I was spun and dragged through the shallow sewer on the mattress as I held on for my life. Every piece of ID and cash was in those bags, so I kept my white-knuckle death grip as I became tired. After disturbing the water, the horrible stench was paralyzing, and sewer solids and water dripped from my face. More dirty people gathered around the tug-of-war and from the looks on their faces, they *weren't* there to join my side of the conflict.

The scene again faded to black as I found myself surrounded. Again, I awoke in the freezing cold and Carlo was sticking the heart monitor sensors back to my chest.

"They came off and it make-a-tha-beeping-sound," Carlo said.

"WHERE IS MY MONEY CARLO?" I yelled.

"Señor, your money is in your bags," Carlo replied in broken English.

"NO, I WANT MY FUCKING BAGS, CARLO! WHO HAS MY BAGS?" I demanded in a state of delirium.

Due to the ataxia, I could barely move.

"You need to take this now," Carlo instructed as he fed me two more pre-measured Ibogaine capsules.

"I will be back, okay?" Carlo asked.

(Though I slipped in and out of those realistic dreams, I still didn't have my bags, and it tortured me. Also, I was allowed to worry about my lack of contact with Katie since I'd been there. I did nothing without Iboga's permission.)

Back into a trance, I fell and, again, the witches in the camper dream beat me to hell as I was tossed around firmly. Then, I found myself back in the video game, crashing into pixels and back into the hot-boxing vision. For lifetimes, I read the basement walls until I became gravely concerned about Katie ditching me over the whole failure. My siblings and I followed faster and faster behind my mother through Times Square, to no avail.

Over-and-again, the same settings randomly barraged me with the same images; it was a nightmare. During this period, I never knew where I would end up, but, it was sure to be one of those horrible places.

The muffled sound of the Little Chef's banging cooking implements woke me from the netherworld. (Those noises would be my only connection to the "this world" during the experience.) When I heard banging on the pans, I would imagine it was daytime again, and when it went silent, I surmised it to be night time. Waking up periodically to either Carlo or Jessica feeding me more pills was part of the routine too.

The nursing schedule was also an indicator of the time of day. Trying to piece the time continuum together using those baselines was futile too. I tried, but it didn't form a distinct pattern. I found myself in the Tijuana Canal again, and then back to the cardboard box cleanse, in Mexico—on and on, the ongoing nonsensical dialectic-cycle continued.

(Waking up soaked in sweat during this part of the experience was the only indicator of detox. There was never any pain or discomfort. It didn't physically hurt, but I was miserable from the brutal mental repetition of that part of it.)

Carlo again approached, and I realized he was holding my bags Excitedly, I swung the upper half of my body toward Carlo with the elegance of Linda Blair in her 1973 film, *The Exorcist*.

"Thank you so much, Carlo."

As I was trying to sit upright, Carlo discouraged me and laid the bags on the bed. After rolling over and feeling for my wallet for several minutes, Carlo finally asked, "Would you like for me to help you, Tim?"

Reluctantly, I answered "yes," only because I couldn't find it on my own. (Walking to the restroom wouldn't have been plausible—the ataxia was disabling—crazy disabling.)

Carlo inserted his hand into the black leather bag and it came right back out with my wallet in it. After stripping the cash, I fanned it in front of my face; it was quite obviously several hundred dollar bills. They were pastel rainbow colors, though, so the counting effort would have proven vain. Satisfied, I tossed the wallet and money to the side after again realizing I had to urinate terribly.

I grabbed for the trash can, which bent with a slight pull when the weight of the piss kept it stationary. Now, I used two hands. Operating carefully to prevent spillage, I managed to get the trash can back to my bedside. The weight of the wastebasket consisted entirely of my urine. While splashing even more fresh pee into the trashcan, the odor overwhelmed me, and I began to gag and heave.

After much ado, I brought up a small amount of thick black matter. My stomach contents tasted like a burnt, earthy gritty concoction. Straining immensely, I squeezed my hands and realized that my motor skills were coming back some. While continuing to vomit, I instinctively knew it was the manifestation of evil leaving my body; the purging felt quite spiritual and was a relief. Deep from within my spirit, I heard a confident voice ask, "Timothy, my son, would you like to die now?"

"Yes, I can't do this anymore. I'm done trying here. I give, I'm finished."

(I wasn't even sad; I had great conviction and peace with my decision.)

12.

The Big Show

Just when I thought it was all over, I was again dragged into dreamland. Faint Native African drumming began while a tribal chief's face hovered before me in midair. Campfire light flickered behind the tribal leader and the drumming increased; this time to a most comfortable level.

The hovering ancestral face had a friendly twinkle in his eye, a ghostly white painted face, and a headdress made from dried brown grass. He offered some cantillation, but, sadly, I didn't understand his tongue. After his chant, the chief's hovering face instantly changed into a blaring electric-orange wooden tiki (or mask-type thing).

With a rotational motion, the tiki lowered, shrunk, interchanged with a journal in my back, and at the same time, a dirty, blackish vertebra was expelled into midair. The rejected vertebra hovered in front of my organism for a few seconds, then just vanished.

An orange juice-type liquid traveled up my spinal cord from the tiki, cooling as the juice stained my spine all the way up to my skull. When the extract reached my brain, it too became saturated with the beautiful orange concoction that resonated with a gleaming photonic brilliance.

God herself made her presence in an instant upon a canvas of bright blue skies. Yes, God was she, what's more *she* looked exactly like my mother when she was 25 years old. At first, I felt her guise as a form of deception, but, I was quickly and silently corrected. God was beautiful, but I could barely look at her without burning my eyes.

Carefully, I took brief peeks until being forced to look away and here is what I saw: A weather system of distortion swarmed God's being like heat waves radiating from a hot barbecue grill. The vibration of a high-voltage transformer buzzed and popped loudly in my ears as a reminder of the sheer force of God's presence, except I could feel the vibration of the heavy bass snapping (the noise sounded like the electric arc of a giant *Tesla Coil,* the gizmos flashing lightning in *Dr. Frankenstein*'s lab).

Once again, we spoke completely silently. God looked at me tellingly, then back up at the sky. A slow, aerial arm motion hummed like a twirling lightsaber with which God ripped the fabric of space-time. A jagged-edged cut was left in midair and the arch-shaped flap of "reality" sagged down, exposing a window of the same shape to black nothingness.

The spectacle was exciting and frightening, but again I felt very safe; I recognized the display as a demonstration of power. Every physical action God made was followed by a clear, colorful rainbow-like sparkly trail that quickly dissipated. The scene faded.

On a grassy, African plain I then found myself. There was no water in the scene. There were cattails, however, to indicate the presence of moisture. Still, I felt God's commanding presence, but I couldn't physically see her standing next to me

Page 174

anymore. Termite mounds and sandstone outcroppings painted the margins. Two large groups of indigenous peoples were standing, one to each side of me. (I was African too, by the way.) Two African bull elephants with tribal leaders mounted upon them lumbered from side to side as they approached one another.

When the biomass of people parted, accommodating the elephant riding chiefs, the two opposing groups had solemn looks on their faces as did their leaders. The elephants spoke using only the eyes, as did their leaders. Fanned ears nearly doubling their head-size showed the elephants to be on a high alert. The two leaders sat fully erect during a long silent exchange before the group erupted.

Dancing, singing, drumming, and visiting ensued as the two groups merged into one, large, happy crowd. Wilding out, I kicked my legs, dancing arm and arm with the clique. I knew every step to every crazy dance and felt impressive to onlookers while doing so. While clapping, the happy mob circled and bounced to my frequency. We fellowshipped, frolicked, and shared ideas. I could see so clearly; the colors were vibrant; the air fresh and the temperature perfect. During the festival, I asked God telepathical-ly, "God, why can't you bring my brother Joey back to me?"

At the kitchen table in the Glendale, Arizona, home in which we lived before my parents divorced, all of the siblings (in-cluding Joey) were there with God. Being the young children we were when living there, we sat at the kitchen table and played with something within the table as God stood above us. My siblings were unaware of God's presence so just continued playing as chil-dren do.

On display within the table was a model of Times Square, and, as I looked closer, the city was complete with tiny miniature people moving in rabbles through the streets. It wasn't a model at all but the actual Times Square. The city was in three-dimensional relief, extending deep inside the table to accommodate the tall buildings within the tabletop. Miniaturized characters, street performers, clean white steam billowing from manholes, cars, trucks, and taxicabs were everywhere.

The vehicles communicated through a series of quick, calculated-honks that echoed amongst the buildings.

God held a small red and silver object in her hand, which she rendered to my little brother who must have been three at the time. God asked Nathan to stick the object anywhere he wanted. Without social engagement, Nathan reached his little hand into the mini NYC and attached the object to the side of a skyscraper. Nathan then went on with his playing.

The object instantly sprouted three different-colored tubes —one green, one purple, and one red. Steam billowed from the flared ends of the pipes. I followed the red tube's path, as all three grew longer and longer, heading down two different streets in two separate directions. The colorful pipes came upon another crossroad and the final tube split. Now, they traveled in three directions, down three unique streets.

As the red pipe headed down a street, a businessman walked in its path, so the pipe made a quick detour around the man and continued along. When looking back, he flashed the look of astonishment. Then the pipe dodged another person, then a whole crowd, and so on, as it continued down the streets of New York City.

I looked at the city as a whole and the colored pipes now clogged the entire scene from top to bottom; every person was bound by the pipes that encapsulated them. The crowds moved their legs but went nowhere since colored tubes now entangled their bodies. God and I made eye contact, and I instantly understood that her bringing Joey back would disrupt the flow of everything else in the universe.

The demonstration seemed very suiting since Joey nearly obsessed with *The Butterfly Effect* when he was alive. (The Butterfly Effect is an example of *Chaos Theory*, which illustrates how small initial differences may lead to large unforeseen consequences over time.) It seemed God knew the perfect thing to communicate with a single action since there was never another question about the same situation.

One scene again faded and another materialized. I was in India and more people were walking all around. There was a profusion of shanty houses built from shipping pallets, tarps, and plastic refuse. The shanty-town was immense, and people aimlessly milled around in the stinky mud. They didn't look miserable from their expressions and didn't seem to have a purpose, yet still seemed happy. They all worked in a large, adjacent trash-dump and dragged key finds back to their burrows. We watched the scene until being teleported into outer space again.

In a space colony, we silently traveled in a floating craft, which traversed through its vacuum streets. A great sense of peace, pride, and unity welled inside me while I quietly spoke with other floating crafts. An internet of information was accessible using only my thoughts, and I gleamed while doing so.

The buildings were enormous, floating, modular structures. We drifted past a glass-faced superstructure with the *Today Show*

Page 177

logo on it where filming took place inside. As we passed the *Today Show* the craft self-tuned to the programming inside the studio. I had the fresh morning feeling of waking up to smiling faces discussing the events of another beautiful day.

There was no land, just a never-ending metropolis of these grand floating structures that looked like skyscrapers placed on their sides. It might have been the distant future and it was gorgeous, so I felt pride for my race. (While gazing through the windows to other worlds, I felt a great sense of oneness as if I were part of a universal movement. The entire time I vacillated between smiling to a shiver and crying my eyes out with joy.)

Having spent time in the distant future, I now found myself in the past. God stood next to me in the face of a towering cliff face. Trapped in the massive rock was the fossil of a T. rex frozen in a fetal death pose. I goggled at the beast as it grew organs, tendons, muscles, and scaly skin. After flexing its newfound muscle, the animal discharged the rock with a thunderous blast; she displayed a semi-circular head-motion and stomped away. There was another fossil of a Stegosaurus right behind her.

The scene repeated over-and-again as we time-traveled through the fossil record. I witnessed every animal ever straying planet Earth in full animation. The dinosaurs displayed shockingly bright colors; even the T. rex had the shading of a tropical bird. Several of the dinosaurs changed colors like a kaleidoscope, closely matching every tree and shrub as they bumbled on their way.

Beasts from every time period of our planet were represented in the geology before me. Stores of humanoids like ourselves came to life, wee ones, even giants but they all varied in some subtle way. I walked miles toward the vanishing cliff side as it eroded into animals from our past. Eventually, the entire mountain of rock came to life and roamed, scurried, and flew away in varied directions.

From there, I floated to an overhead view of many different varieties of terrain. Some were rocky, others watery, and many were intermingled with temporary icy expansions. I witnessed great migrations of animals, humanoids, and even the plant and insect kingdoms as they traveled around the planet.

Plants were cognizant and communicated readily. After earning their trust; I came to appreciate their humor that was satirical but affectionate. Their initial sarcasm was the result of years of dismissal and disrespect by humanoids. They didn't mind the sacrifices made for the humanoids, but they thought they deserved more credit.

No longer using their natural medicines also left them bitter; they felt as if we had turned our backs on the plants. In a way, the plants got to live through humanoids. But, we had orphaned them. After explaining my shifting view of the potential of plant medicine, the demeanor of the plants also altered; they felt useful, I could tell. Plants were cuddly creatures by nature and their dispositions suited them well, considering their tactile living habits. (We humans just don't usually possess the sensory tools in which to communicate in those ways.)

There were many coincidental, symbiotic migration routes that were a voluminous terrestrial Noah's Ark, an aggregate of biological diversity. As one mass, people, beast, fowl, and plant all utilized small strips of geo-bridge, like ancient highways, through magical lands. The land bridges mostly connected desirable migration routes. All of the organisms knew of seasonal, geographic resources with which to sustain themselves along their trip.

During the great exodus, there were times of lean where death prevailed, and yet others, when a feeling of hope and adventure flourished. Most of the plants just hitched rides as seeds in the fur of beasts, but some of the migrations occurred with no symbiotic mobility mechanism at all. Those plants traveled independently via the wind, animal feces, and root-running. Though slow, over time their movements proved deliberate and practical.

There were many vivid scenes of different beautiful couples running and frolicking. One such couple ran through a field of a tall grassy crop showing lovely hues of green. Shiny waxy leaves worshiped the sunlight while gusts announced their presence with the fateful harvest's graceful shimmy.

The handsome young man chased his mate past a pair of muscular beasts of burden, which were yoked and worked the land. The animals bore a pungent earthy musk, which was not unpleasant. The slender blonde woman baring much skin turned her head in slow motion as she ran from her suitor; her hair flowed slowly, masking a smile. Then, my mind flashed to many other similar scenes occurring in yet different settings and times, but like this one, passionate young couples larked.

Now aboard an ancient ship along with many others, we slowly glided through an archaic harbor where the people on its coastline appeared to flourish. Music of the likes I've never heard, echoed in the safety of the crescent-shaped port. The hopeful people lived in harmony. The harbor water's unclouded depth revealed much sea-life. Approaching countless ancient ports, in their days of glory, made the ship passengers' monumental importance to the history of humankind inherently known.

I came-to in the basement room where Jessica was again holding the Gatorade straw to my mouth.

"You should be getting almost better now, Timoteo," Jessica said.

When smiling back, I felt compelled to share the gorgeous things I'd seen. The secrets of the universe were contained deep inside of me, but I couldn't yet tell anyone. In my unstable mental state, I attempted to explain things to Jessica but knew they weren't coming out right. After a single sentence of crazy, I realized I would've needed my whole life only to explain that one scene.

"No, Mijo, you are not quite done, yet," Jessica said with a giggle.

Now, there was absolutely no fear. That was my favorite part because there was no more agony or torture, only the most profound revelations. I had a personal relationship with God that I had never felt in my life. Even with eyes open, I could feel her presence within everything. Though mind-numbing, I wanted it over with so I could share my secrets, but I was still excited to see what the next vision held.

The wind passed through my hair as I now found myself physically standing at the edge of a cliff overlooking a grand canyon. It was deeper and greater than the Grand Canyon back in Arizona, and this one was more monstrous. I could barely see the other side. A dark sun contorted to peek around every angle of the mountains in the distance. It felt like the dawn of time. I gazed upon the abyss.

Clear, glass elevators stretched from one end of the expanse to the other, in both directions. They all had four walls of thick spotless glass and were pieced together by shiny silver hardware, like the fancy showers in Las Vegas. The elevators were stacked and connected by bright, silver chains that were spiral-shaped, sterling silver models of the nucleic acid, double helix. The chains attached each elevator, one-to-another. The endless rotation of the helical chains raised the elevators as they turned while the glimmering silver-hardware sparkled. The sea of shiny "Archimedes' screws" muscled its humanoid bounty from our Earth, and did so with a great grinding moan.

The elevators' simple but ornate construction was in the mechanical style of the late 1800s. The elevators again moaned and after stopping, the glass doors flung open and a proliferation of naked humankind walked out of the elevators and replenished the Earth.

Carefully leaning into the chasm, I could see the chain of elevators, filling the canyon, in every direction. The immaculate and glittery elevators crammed the void. Each lighted glass elevator in the dark hole contained a single inanimate human being. The second the persons exited the glass chambers, the top level just vanished. Every other string of elevators had an individual of different sex inside, each of whom varied in color and race.

In an endless march, the elevators advanced and another throng animated and walked out from the sea of elevators. The multitude of nude humans walked in all directions through the air until they met land. When the humans reached land, they continued walking until vanishing in the darkening distance. I watched what must have been billions of people spill out from the hole, from deep inside the earth and wondered what was taking place.

I didn't recognize any of them until I looked down and saw my grandfather in the next elevator. When my step-grandpa wasn't around, Grandma Zigler always said, "You look so handsome, just like Grandpa Lewis!" It was one of her guilty indulgences.

I only knew Grandpa Lewis from pictures because we all knew "not to discuss Grandpa Lewis" – most likely, a rule grandpa

Zigler had made. (Remember? My real grandfather was allegedly hung to death in that gas station restroom by my step-grandfather.)

My father was in the subsequent elevator. Finally, I saw me, along with my family and children step out from those shiny elevators. My dad, who was naked (everyone was nude), stood next to me for a moment, and then walked me into the next scene. Looking at the ocean, my father and I (now both clothed) casually strolled along a quaint seaside setting. Single-level buildings, all constructed in the arts and crafts style, were built of unpainted, roughly sawn wood. All of the stores and shops were connected into one long structure which faced the ocean. All of the shops shared a long tin-roof, as well as a large front porch, which served as an extended walkway for the turn of the century style strip mall. The entire concourse faced the ocean and the setting was beautiful. There were wooden barrels banded with steel, as well as wooden benches spaced every-so-often. My father was very fond of antiques, as well as period architecture. We could see and hear the ocean from the concourse as we wandered through the shops. Clop-clop, our feet stomped along the old, wooden floor.

My father also loved the ocean, and we could smell its damp, salty stench as we walked and silently visited. We looked into the shop windows and around the seascape, as my father pointed out items, and birds of interest, or what he thought looked "cool." It was a menagerie of his favorite things, and as we walked the wooden decking, it wrapped around the end of the mall.

There were more wooden benches built into the handrails of a circular area of the concourse, which served as a resting area. There was a round hole sawn into the center of the sitting area floor deck, which served as a planter. A large, old, oak tree grew from the planter in the heart of the wooden walkway.

We sat on a wooden bench, and tears streamed down our long faces, but I couldn't understand what Dad had said. I focused intently, but it was no use. My father pointed up to a carved piece of wood detail at the top of the wooden-arched entrance to the sitting area. My eyes tracked his finger up to a wonderfully carved, wood scrolling, which too was unpainted.

There were antique glass bottles placed into carefully hewn voids, and the bottles fit perfectly inside of them. It had a folk-art look, but was symmetrical, neat, and just worked. Colorful antique glass bottles shone in a sun, which now threatened us with the full show.

A wind chime tinkled in the distance as I wiped a tear from Dad's eye; we now both smiled and gazed up at the woodcarving through teary eyes. When I looked back at Dad, he was gone, and I sobbed. Again, I glanced at the weathered carving, alone this time, and the wood was aged and rotten.

Only splintered fragments of the now weathered wooden ornament remained, but the bottles were still intact. The sun came out in time to spill rainbow-colored light slivers on the broken-down building. The oak tree was dead and rotten, as was the entire mall, and a scared feeling owned me as the scene came to a close.

I began to wonder where people go when they perish. God and I, again, shared the view of our Earth from outer-space. A large, egg-shaped, aura-like membrane encompassed our blue planet. The large, more-rounded end of the "egg shape" fit the bottom of our planet, entirely. The pointy end of the egg shape was face up, leaving an atmospheric void. The aura was a thin, ultraviolet-spectrum colored veil, which looked much like the skin of a bubble.

Violet, blue, and red rainbows, in the veil's skin, swirled slowly in the sun. The aura served as a barrier to our Earth and countless small flashes of light, in the same ultraviolet spectrum, darted into the aura with no certain pattern or timing; I knew them to be souls, or "love." I'm calling them: *Electric Love.*

My view quickly changed to that of a helicopter, hovering at a fast clip forward, just above the ocean's skin, as saltwater quickly passed by my view. At once, a playful dolphin breached the water with a leap and quickly matched the pace of my new view of the water that passed by. After chasing the dolphin, a small, colorful dart of electric love was swimming alongside the animal. The light reminded me of those tropical "tetra" fish when carving tight maneuvers beside the dolphin until leaping inside of it.

The electric love then took control of the dolphin, operating it as its own organism until catching up with several more darts of the same light, or love. The original light leaped back out of the animal just in time to join the static group of lights. The several lights conversed silently just as God and I had throughout the entire experience.

13.

Reanimation

God and I were in total darkness, and merely existing with no physical body and she silently asked, "Do you still want to die, Timothy? If you are still willing, I will happily grant you your wish."

I thought about Katie, my girls, and all the beautiful things I'd seen. I thought about the incredible life I had at home. Life could now be lived, without the need for a chemical, the way God had intended me to live. The good outweighed the bad. As a matter of fact, the soul already longed to rejoin the "this world."

I lived in a beautiful house, in a part of the world where there was plenty. There was work for those who wanted it. I had clean clothes, nice cars, and many other material things, which no longer seemed to matter to me anymore. Before God had mentioned it again, I had almost forgotten about my prior decision to die.

Guilt overwhelmed me for trying to kill myself for so many years. Now I saw both life and addiction for what they were. Life was a short but beautiful experience in which to enjoy and learn from, and certain drugs were death, despair, and masked all of the uncertainties we perceive as fear. I knew not to spend another day concerned with the moment I or anyone else would expire, and I no longer wished to waste any time that could be spent enjoying myself and the survivors.

Addiction became a mindless action that I had repeated with no awareness of its harm to my body and mind, just as my foolish, little green video-game avatar crashed over-and-over again into those green pixels. Every bit of romance that I had ever had for the drug had magically transformed into hate, and the dope hungry monster within seemed to have lost his ugly voice. I reflected upon the live or die option: That option must be responsible for the 1/300 death rate, I concluded. The weighty sensation of profound discovery tugged at my soul.

Those patients who had died had had a choice and chose to die, I reveled. I took a moment to feel sorrow for people not having enough to justify their stay in the "this world." Here I've been clean for what amounted to a couple of days, and comically I have already reclassified myself as "clean," I thought. I snickered as if I had gotten away with something unbelievable. (With most detox methods I would have been just beginning the worst of the physical and mental thrashing.) My skin felt cold from within and to the touch, and my motor skills were coming back too. I couldn't wait to experience our planet with my new organism, and I also needed to call Katie. She must be so worried or did she just think that I had abandoned her and the kids? (Cue: horribly, shitty, guilty, feeling again.)

I had now been awake for who knows how long yet I still felt rested, spiritually charged, and ready to go. When trying to roll over, I realized that I still couldn't move one hundred percent.

There was a feeling that no one had been there to check on me for days, though, I knew that probably wasn't true. Though I still couldn't figure out how to crawl out of bed, I was beginning to regain my faculties.

As I lie half on my side, some light from underneath my back caught my attention. When I rolled over, even more, I revealed a round, metallic hatch, with a white bushing of lighted plastic as a jamb, which looked like a hatch from a space colony. I was fully awake and cognizant while witnessing the vision with eyes open, and in the "this world."

It was dark in the room, other than the green monitor's glow and the lighted hatch-grommet. The round hatch flipped open spastically as I watched an orange spot the size of a basketball pop out from the round portal. There was cold-steam, similar to that which is emitted by dry ice when submerged in a punch bowl, rising from the opening. A thick, white beam of light, reaching to the ceiling of the dark room, highlighted the smoke. A burnt, oaky smell lingered in the air.

The orange spot had a purple tone, which radiated and fluttered throughout the orange to express its mood. The colored spot's outer-edge shook an orange-purple fur when it scurried around and settled back into a solid orange when still. The orange and purple hues would sometimes ripple outward in waves toward the spot's circumference, reminding me of a manta ray flying through the water. He was nothing more than a two-dimensional spot of orange color, but he had more personality than anyone I knew.

He didn't stand still for very long, and I quickly realized that the *Tang*-orange, colored spot followed my every move.

When I moved an inch, after a fraction of a second delay, my new friend would immediately join me, just the inch away.

Plainly, I must have forgotten my buddy in the other world, and it was certainly nice of the spirits to let him back through, I thought. It seemed my new orange friend was there to guide us safely back into the "this world," and he did; it was awesome because lonely feelings faded. The shaft of light disappeared as the hatch slammed shut with a lusty metallic bang, but "Tang" was still as bright as ever. The absent portion of bed materialized where the hatch once was, and Tang was more-pronounced in the dark, like a sunspot in the eyes after staring at our star. Suddenly, the door to my room opened and John, Grady, and Jessica all busted in with excitement.

"Did you see it?" Grady happily asked, as if there were an expected outcome of events.

After a body roll had revealed my bright-orange spot to the group, I said, "Yes, I saw it. Here he is." I felt my spot smile at the group and me.

I smiled back, and Tang eagerly scurried back underneath me where he belonged and felt most safe. A purply-orange happy vibration fluttered. Wearing the same proud smile, I again gladly looked up at the crowd after the demonstration.

"What are you doing, bro?" Grady asked, as the entire group laughed.

(I didn't take it personally since I realized they just weren't seeing what I was.)

A sense of wisdom, of seeing the big picture, and being confident with my being resonated within me.

"Dude, I was asking if you got the feeling of oneness, or one, like everyone feels?" Grady better articulated.

Oh my God, I do think differently, I thought. (I ignored Grady as if he hadn't uttered a word. We weren't on the same level.) I felt empathy for their lack of understanding, and no ill will toward the group for laughing at me. Holy cow! What did I read on those walls? I so deeply pondered.

"I want to get up and see the world," I begged the group.

"You're not finished yet, dude. Almost," Grady assured, as the whole team reinforced his judgment.

"You will go through an intense reflection stage now," Grady said.

"How long have I been under?"

"Well, let's see here, it's about 2:00 PM, so you've been down for around 27 hours," Grady said.

"OH MY GOD I HAVE TO CALL KATIE," I suddenly shouted.

"We have everything taken care of, Timmy; she knows you're fine. You are in no condition to call anyone so just get up on your own time," Grady said.

"Guys, I have never felt better; I want to get up now," I pleaded. They all wore happy and proud looks upon their faces.

"What?" I asked the group with a smile.

"DUDE, YOU DID IT, BRO," Grady exclaimed, as they all celebrated, each issuing me a high five.

"You're clean, man," Grady praised.

A tear welled up and rolled down my cheek as the greatest sense of pride engulfed my being. The crew had initiated me into the coolest club on our planet. The tears hurt, as in pain; they physically hurt. (Having not cried for nearly ten years, I'd forgotten how it had felt, and I marveled that crying caused physical pain.) Taking a personal second to enjoy the unusually nice release at the end, I welled up as the tear rolled down my face. (When you learn these things as a child, they are new, and thus bear no real significance; it is just "crying." When you get it back for the second time, as a forty-year-old man, it is different.)

I was the hero in my very own science fiction movie. My story was no different from that of say, Pinocchio's, or David's, from the film AI. Grady was right; I didn't wake up in a tub of ice with incisions where my kidneys once were. I wasn't tortured, beaten, or sold into human slavery; I was a real man again, I thought.

"Get some rest, playboy," Grady said as the group exited the room.

Grady casually flipped the light back on as the group exited the little room while excitedly mumbling.

As a new puppy left at home alone for the very first time, longingly, I stared at the closed door out of which the group had just exited. I heard faint laughs from the group; the workers must be happy for their time off, I thought. After all, the patients (Wayne and I) had been under for nearly a day-and-a-half. The collateral smells of Chef's dinner routine began creeping under my door.

Much of that time was spent reflecting upon my travels as the smells and sounds of normal life once again beckoned me. Many times I attempted to stand, and the first several didn't go well since I just stared into space, with my feet dangling off the bed. But by the fourth or fifth time, I managed to stand up.

My mind determined the room to be cluttered, though a scan deemed it clean save for the sweet aroma of rotten piss and two-and-a-half dozen or so C-notes that laid scattered about the bed and floor. My bags still laid on the bed behind me, and I had a flashback of actually embracing the duffle like it was a human being at one point. Developed and reprogrammed with the knowledge I needed for fully appreciating the human experience, I proceeded.

I was truly born-again. I was cleansed and rebuilt from the soul up by God herself, aside from the stiffness. Wearing the face of optimism, carefully placing one foot in front of the other, I waddled past the hundred-dollar bills and approached the door. When at the bedroom door, I conducted a body scan to ensure that I looked proper for the group.

Wearing pajama pants, I was shirtless, my emergency-port wraps had come partially unwound, leaving an ace bandage to dangle by my side, and my hair was cats-assed. I need a shirt, I thought. I produced a plain white T-shirt from my bag and stretched it over my head. I shuffled my way back to the door and stood there for a second. Okay, there, I'm good now, I thought, after giving myself another glance.

Finally, I twisted the knob and cracked the bedroom door, to reveal the brightest lemon-yellow light in the world. The sun burned my eyes intensely. I slammed the door shut and closed my eyes again to rest them. Forcing my eyes back open, little-by-little, I again revealed the giant golden ball of plasma which hovered just above the Pacific Ocean.

The bright, controlled explosion was reflecting, glimmering, and dancing with the movement of the waves, back toward the rocky beach. The ocean magnified our star's great girth so effectively it hurt.

As my eyes continued to adjust, a large, plate-glass wall spanning along the back of the house came into focus, which maximized the view of the ocean. It was a basement level apartment, which also opened up to the sea. Having flashbacks of men carrying me downstairs made me realize that I was standing in a lower-level of a great, ocean-side cliff-dwelling.

A scan of the room revealed the large, dimly lit stone stairway on which the team brought me to that subterranean dungeon, before the treatment. Butterflies churned my stomach. Carefully I moved clockwise up the cold spiral steps as they transported me to the main level of the structure. As I ascended, I heard the sounds of life, laughter, and music growing louder.

The soul of Eddie Vedder's masterpiece, *Guaranteed*, was heard and felt as I slowly emerged.

Another tear streamed my face while exiting the grotto.

Walking down the hall past the kitchen, the dining room, and eventually the living room, I made my way back into life. The familiar orange-yellow glow crept through the air as our sun's powerful evening program beamed through the viewing window. When I arrived in the living room, everyone paused and looked up at me.

Isabelle and Tiffany clutched packed bags, but instantly dropped them and screamed upon noticing me.

"You are shell-shocked, but you look fucking great, Tim," Tiffany said.

"Yes," Isabelle eagerly added, smilingly.

"Oh my God, I wish I could hear all about it," Tiffany said.

"Yes," Isabelle again agreed.

"We are leaving now, and I wish all of the best for you, Tim. That was fun," Tiffany said.

Tiffany gave me one last high-5 and headed down the hall.

Isabelle said some heartfelt words and, after another quick hug, she ran to catch up, joining her new friend. There were chill bumps as Vedder hummed the end; the first track from the same album began playing, and the lyrics seemed fitting. There I stood, with a blank, expressionless look on my face. Grady and John approached me. (Now, I felt unable to respond to the girls. I knew then that I might have gotten up a little early.)

"Dude, I can't believe that you're even up," Grady said.

"What time is it, Grady?" I asked.

"Oh, it's About 5:20," Grady answered. I mentally noted that I had been under for roughly 30 hours.

"I think it's the soonest I've ever seen anyone get out of bed on their own. You, John?"

"Same. You're doing great, Tim," John encouraged.

"Can I go outside and see the ocean?" I asked of the two.

"Sure," Grady said as he led the way.

The infamous glass sliding door that led to the back porch now seemed to be permanently stuck open.

"Oh my God, that is gorgeous!" I couldn't speak very well yet.

(It felt like I had a mouth full of pea gravel.) The two men bobbled their heads up-and-down exaggeratedly in agreement as the three of us enjoyed the sunset. They seemed to avoid eye contact to avoid the creep-out factor, and there was none. But, I appreciated the gesture as the men lit cigarettes. It felt like another vision.

Again, my mouth turned up at its corners to reveal a huge smile and an elevated sense of mood became intense as God herself again spoke silently.

"Hey, I'll have one of those," I said to Grady.

"NO CIGRITS, NO CIGRITS," Grady commanded loudly.

I think Grady was trying to say: "no cig-a-rettes," but was far too excited to pronounce the whole thing. Grady seemed to care about my well-being.

"You should quit smoking, too, Timmy. Take advantage of this opportunity," Grady said.

"How do you feel now?" John asked.

"Um, I feel like a horse kicked me in the head. I don't hurt. I just feel like a horse kicked me in my head, and everything I knew flew right out my ear."

"HA - HA - HA," the two men laughed.

"It should all come back to you by the end of the week," John said.

(I wondered if "it" would ever "all come back to me," but I felt fine.)

"What all did you see in there, Timmy?" Grady asked.

"Oh my God, guys, I met God, and she was a woman. I saw my birth, life, death, and my body decaying into nothing. I saw dinosaurs too and…."

I finished speaking before I was really through because I couldn't correctly put the experience into words.

"I know, I know, enough said," Grady exclaimed.

"What were you trying to show us when you moved over in the bed a little bit ago?" Grady asked while making sly eye contact with John.

I quickly looked down at my feet and took a step to my right to make room for the possibility that they could now see my new friend.

"Look, I know that you can't see him, guys, but there's an orange friend that follows me everywhere I go."

Page 196

As I looked down, I noticed a faded version of the orange spot that had scurried back beneath my feet, and realized that my companion was fading from the "this world." I asked the guys a question. "How long do you think that this feeling will last? I feel better than ever."

"Oh, it should last about a month, then you should start feeling normal again," John assured.

How is that plausible? I wondered. I felt like a teenager again, except with more optimism and eagerness to explore the world.

"Hey, Timmy, you wanna go for a little car ride?" Grady asked.

"Is that okay, Grady? I would love to," I answered.

"Let's go then, player," Grady said as he walked down the hall toward the front door.

Still stiff, and in stocking-feet, I tried my best to follow Grady until we arrived at the car.

"Can I just wear this?" I asked.

"I don't see why not. You're not gonna run into your friends, are you?" Grady asked laughingly.

"Besides, we're going to fucking Wal-Mart, so you're already dressed quite appropriately," Grady quipped.

As I exited the front door, I looked back at the house, and did a double-take; the entire house was green instead of yellow.

The car was a gray Korean-model rental, which sat curbside in front of the house; I hopped in, and the car sped off. As Grady and I exited the gate to the subdivision, I noticed a rusty, old, iron billboard with a picture of The Donald plastered to it. Donald Trump was faded, partially peeled up at a corner, and covered in seagull shit.

We hung a right and barreled Southbound down the Mexican PCH. It was nearly dark, but I could still see the last few minutes of sunlight glowing across the Pacific. My arms rested at my sides helplessly as I started to feel somewhat tired.

"Why is *Donald Trump*'s picture on that billboard?" I asked Grady as he nervously puffed on his electric cigarette.

"Well, I don't know all of the details, Timmy, but, I do know he started building on the ocean, here. Actually, I think that's the spot, there," Grady quickly pointed out.

"I guess it was supposed to be the Trump Towers en Tijuana, but it ate his lunch, aye. For some reason, construction halted, Trump left town and that there is all that's left. Well, other than broken dreams and squandered retirement money. I guess I can't honestly say what happened there, Timmy. But whatever it was, it doesn't look good, right?" Grady finished.

"I suppose you're right, Grady," I agreed.

As we drove south, I saw half-built skyscrapers sprouting from the cliffs and beaches along the way. There were large, rusted iron skeletons, many with glass facades extending only halfway up their exteriors and no job trailers or materials sat beside them to indicate construction anymore. The heavy equipment scarred landscape already eroded from lack of maintenance, and there were no tractors there to do that maintenance. Hurricane fencing surrounded some of the lots but had been knocked down and graffiti tagging embellished the marble facade at the base of one of the intended hotel resorts.

Construction of those great monoliths of modern marvel must have begun during unquestionably better times. They stood guard, their rusty backs to the ocean like the giant *Moai Statues* of *Easter Island*. They were far larger, though, and the bright golden

Page 198

streak of twilight eerily backlit the Gods. What a shame that these towering monuments just stand there vacant, I thought to myself. (Had I just fallen into another vision? Would the line between perception and reality ever have a crisp boundary again? I wondered.)

I saw shanty neighborhoods that looked a lot like the Eastern-Indian ones from my trip along the way, and I gasped at them. While watching dark shadows of people moving about, I loudly verbalized, "The misery."

"Come again?" Grady asked.

In-tune with the fact that he wasn't following my lead, I said nothing more. Grady quickly turned his attention back toward the road. He had apparently recognized my outburst as a side effect of the medicine, and therefore, ignored it. The road nearly hypnotized me as I pondered the crazy riddle which was posed to me by the witches in the camper, from my visions....*What did that mean?*

14.

Mental Ward Escapee

After rather enjoying the apocalyptic landscape for a half-hour or so, we dipped into a large parking lot. A grande white bulb-lit sign that flashed, *JACKPOT*, marked the ingress of the property. Grady wheeled around to the back lot of the *Casino Jackpot*, exposing that industrial giant, *Wal-Mart*. Grady dropped me off at the front door of the megastore.

While he parked the car, I looked down at myself with the stark realization that I had just seen the ends of our Earth and beyond. I frequented heaven and hell, met God and satan, and traveled to different universes and dimensions. I had witnessed wars, destruction, misery, and ultimately re-creation, and then I saw it all happen again, and again, to no end.

All the secrets of the universe had been revealed to me in less than two days' time, and there I stood at the gates of Wal-Mart, of all places, looking like a mental ward escapee. My emergency port wrappings had become partially unwound on my right hand, and I was still in my stocking feet.

Grady pushed a "grocery buggy" through the front doors while I again followed. To my dismay, Grady was right; no one offered me a second glance when walking into the store. However, it looked completely alien to me. I lie. Though the products inside Wal-Mart were entirely different, the actual Wal-Mart in Tijuana, astonishingly, looked mostly the same as the one in Scottsdale. (I'm sure my jammy get-up looked considerably less alien to the locals than what I normally would be wearing in Scottsdale.) When walking along, I looked down at Tang (my orange spot) and smiled; he smiled back. He was even more faded, and it made me want to cry. Grady told me, "Dude, grab anything you want," but food was the very last thing on my mind at that time.

Grady studied a few labels and lobbed about a half cart's worth of groceries into the basket until ending up at the deli counter. There before us, in the glass case, sat a half-carved ham and a worker sliced away at it, underneath a ham lamp. The orange glow of the ham lamp initially threw me into a flashback of the "hot box."

As the man sliced away at the ham, it appeared as if the ham melted away from the chunk of meat rather than falling off in the usual "slices." When the deli worker was done slicing, melting rather, he handed Grady a baggie of "meat" as his knife appeared to drip the bright-red goo.

"This shit is great," Grady celebrated.

"You can have as much of it as you want, Timmy. "

"Okay, thank you, I will," I quietly responded.

I began to detect some unsteady nerves, but they were nothing I couldn't handle. Still I had the fantastic attitude, and no other signs of withdrawal were present.

"How is Wayne doing?" I asked Grady as we headed back to camp in the rental car.

"Oh boy, Timmy, he isn't doing nearly as good as you are," Grady said disappointedly.

"Oh, no!"

"Yeah, well, he is sixty-five years old, Timmy; you've gotta remember that. And, you remember how he handled that DMT experience, right? We knew from that moment we had our hands full with old Wayne, so we administered the Xanax from jump street, but he is doing very well, considering, Timmy. He's opened his eyes now, and John said he's about to get up."

I felt relieved. If the truth be told, I had been looking forward to Wayne's rising. I wondered if Wayne had seen and heard what I had. I knew now, though, that he probably hadn't, due to the Xanax.

Grady and I carried the groceries in and I took a seat in the living room. It was a huge relief knowing the treatment was over with, and I could now begin to piece my life back together.

"Oh no, I need to call Katie," I shouted at the two.

"Um, about that, you are probably in no condition to call your wife yet," John said.

I wanted to talk to Katie, but now that he had mentioned it, I don't know what I would have said to her because it would have all just sounded so crazy right then.

Okay, maybe it wasn't quite over yet.

"Wait a minute. Katie's texting me right now," John said as he read, "'John, I totally want to respect the process, but it has been almost two days since I've heard from Tim or anyone there for that matter. Please have Tim give me a call because I am worried sick.' She is concerned about you, bro. How about you text her from my phone?" John relented.

"That sounds great, John. Let's text her."

John handed me his phone, and I texted, "Katie, it's me. I am overwhelmed right now. Call tomorrow. Tim."

I breathed a sigh of relief since Katie would now know that I was okay. When I was in the experience, the two men promised me that they'd "had it all taken care of," which made me furious inside. Oh well, I thought. Katie knew I was okay, and that's all that mattered. Somehow I didn't realize how outlandish it was to expect that a text from John's phone would lend any validity to our pathetic attempt at a "sign of life."

Things weren't exactly organized at Ibogaine University but, I must say, I liked it that way. My whole life had centered around chaos and instability, and those people were no different. Seeing unique individuals who were just like me, bettering themselves through offbeat means was critical to my recovery.

We are taught as a society that if you don't fit into the same mold as everyone else, then you're somehow inferior to your peers. You're a lowlife or a reject; you don't belong. Rogue, self-thinking, adventurous citizens just like me have one choice in which to recover in the states. That choice? Go to rehab and learn to conform, to be like everyone else. That is perhaps the hardest part of recovery for people like us.

We aren't like them. We never will be, and you can see it all over the faces of those who are desperate enough to be downtrodden by our society's methods for recovery from addiction. They are almost a reprogramming facility in which the government gets ahold of our minds again, feeds us more opiates disguised as miracle drugs that poison our thoughts with mediocrity. We are also taught to reject holistic and shamanistic medicine, which I now know to be another out-and-out lie.

I felt an amazing fellowship. We were a brotherhood of successful and functional misfits and outcasts; the ones who got away. We were self-alienators from an omnipotent *medicine*, scalers of the walls, both literal and figurative. We were living in a commune for a common cause.

A dark feeling of having been deceived by my own people came over me. That deceit was at the cost of death for so many in our country. I could now see so clearly past all of the lies and bull-shit. Even the *1/300 mortality rate* must be a lie. If all of this is also a lie, why wouldn't that be? I felt like I was in the twilight zone or a dream that I would soon wake from, but, I didn't. It was real. It was all real.

Carlo and Jessica told stories, which almost even seemed like myths to the younger helpers who were milling about the fa-cility. Stories of being innocent, young Mexican children who admired the US and what we stood for.

They told stories of being bussed from their schools to San Diego, to *Balboa Park*, to see the museums and all of the wonder that our beautiful, 'colorblind,' free country holds. Every school in Tijuana used to take part in the activity. They marveled in the things that had brought our ancestors here and they still believed in the American dream.

Those wonders no longer existed to their school children, for they were no longer bussed to America. When they told stories of those field trips of long ago, it was akin to *Narnia*, Santa's Workshop, or landing on the moon, to the younger helpers. Amer-ica was an unobtainable world that the 'terrorists' had ruined for them during 9-11. They revered us and our culture, despite what they knew about America's chemical oppression.

They wanted to believe in the American dream so badly that they just accepted the fate they had been dealt. Even though they saw the tail end of the *American nightmare*, first hand, with two new patients every week.

Nurse Jessica approached me at the couch and hugged my neck.

"So proud, I have to go now. Okay? Carlo is here for you tonight."

Carlo forced a small wave and flashed a genuine smile from just behind Jessica.

"Hi, Carlo," I said happily.

I could tell that all the people there could sense a real change in me since I had been up and about. The helpers were more eager to interact and communicate with me now than before the treatment. They knew the evil medicine had robbed our souls. They also knew that their all natural, overnight cure would save my life and change my mind in ways never before thought imaginable.

Looking back, they all seemed to anticipate and then embrace that change in me. Back in the states, recovery patients just sit around and wonder, is it going to work this time? Those helpers knew Ibogaine would work with the execution of a tumor removal. They must have seen this magic trick a thousand times before, I thought. These people just knew their patients were going to shift in every way, for the better.

After the treatment, even the help who spoke no English made eye contact while attempting to communicate through the Mexican charades. There were also random hugs from everyone there. They knew I had been through a lot. They also knew I was there to change my life. It was apparent that they all instinctively sensed that I was now a better person. Jessica disappeared down the hallway.

"You look more better now," Carlo noted.

"I feel 'more better' too, Carlo," I mimicked with a grin.

I could tell that these people had great respect and admiration for Ibogaine and how could they not? If you saw countless numbers of derelict, hopeless drug addicts not only be healed instantaneously, but also just become better people, overnight, how could they not?

"I'm going to do the Ibogaine one day," Carlo boasted quietly.

"You are a drug addict, Carlo?" I silently asked.

"No," Carlo corrected. "I just see how amazing it is for the people in their lifes, and I want to see that too."

The workers watched distressed and malevolent human beings hatch into kind and enlightened creatures. Their patients glowed with a zest for life in three days, after being so ill that they were circling the drain.

Those beautiful Mexican people helped to facilitate those miracles every week. Why wouldn't they want to undergo treatment themselves? I again wondered. It was striking how enlightened and accepting they all were to a process that wasn't even legal in the US and for that I was instantly angry at the terrible ignorance of my country, even then.

Those Mexican people forged a living by saving the lives of the arrogant white country that poisoned its own people, disguising that poison as medicine. The Americans, who had thought they were saving and policing the rest of the world, were being killed off by the stadium load by their own leaders and caretakers, every year.

We were rejected and demonized on our way down the drain too, as if we were flawed; like the merciless mental institutions of yesteryear where homosexuals and indignant wives were sent.

I knew that many people had claimed that drug companies lied about the dangers of opiates. *Many* believed that *our* government doctors were then paid great quantities of money to help spread those lies and hide the truth about the dangers of those drugs. And now that I knew that they were hiding the cure to opiate addiction from the American people, *I* knew these things to be true.

I began to wonder if the people who we pay, to protect us, actually were killing us and our kids for personal gain, instead.

(Perspective is a hell of a thing, is it not?)

I was truly a new creature for the second time in my life. The mental place where I used to check in and see if I was high enough every twenty minutes had turned into a place where I now checked in to see how great I felt naturally. The "mental check-in," was now followed by a sense of pride and an intensive giving of thanks.

Besides the joy that my three girls gave me, being instantaneously free from deadly amounts of opiates was the best feeling in the world.

That mental dumping ground, where I would historically discard any mental garbage I no longer wished to deal with, also seemed to have just vanished. Astonishingly, I had a great sense of any guilt or shame from the past being completely resolved. You could debate and hammer an idea into someone's head for lifetimes and ego alone wouldn't allow that person to accept the notion if it went against programmed beliefs. Here, my whole belief system

Page 208

had been completely reorganized, and my coping mechanisms had been reset in only days.

Somehow, I was now mentally free from all of the idealistic bullshit of our society. Those black veils had indeed been lifted from my eyes, on every topic. I looked forward to reevaluating everything I knew, from a new and more open-minded perspective. John did mention that I would feel "like this" for a month or so.

Hmmm... I further puzzled. Only time would tell if those thoughts would carry on, back home.

Carlo left me in the living room by myself. As I looked around the house, I realized that the help was gone. Everyone else was winding down and preparing for bed. Just then, Wayne's door creaked open slowly. "Hi, Wayne."

(I was relieved to see Wayne's face.)

"Hi, Tim, how are you doing?"

"I am doing good, man. I've been up for hours already, uh, I suppose I've actually been up for days," I replied while scratching my head.

"How are you, Wayne? That is the question."

"I'm doing good too, Tim. It is all very weird," Wayne kept saying as if his mind was skipping like a record.

(Wayne was still in his pajamas.)

"Did that work for you, Tim?"

"Maybe it's just too soon to tell, Wayne, but other than some mental glitches and being a little tired, I feel fine. I feel better than I have in a really long time. No withdrawal, no cravings, just excitement for trying out my new life, Wayne." I paused.

"You, Wayne?"

"Yeah, no, no-cravings, very weird."

Wayne continued. "Yeah, normally I would be on the floor shaking and vomiting right now. I don't know what to make of all of this yet, Tim."

"Did you have any of the visions, Wayne?"

"No, bud, I mean, I might have had one or two really strange things happen, but that's it. Did you?" Wayne asked.

"Visions wouldn't adequately explain what happened, Wayne. I traveled into the past, the future, to heaven and hell, it was crazy. "

I knew not to elaborate too much since Wayne didn't have the same experience as I did; my social barometer was finally correcting itself.

"Well, at least, it worked, right, Wayne?"

"Maybe it's too early to tell, Tim, but yeah, I think you're right, so crazy," Wayne again remarked, as he massaged his own temples with his thumbs.

"Do you wanna go out and have a cigarette, Wayne?"

"Yeah sure, but I didn't even know that you smoked, Tim."

"Yeah, sadly, I do, did. I have an electronic cigarette in my bag that I've been trying to use for a couple of weeks, but it took a shit, so, fuck it."

The two of us walked out and enjoyed a smoke together.

"Wayne, are you tired?"

"No, not really, Tim. I feel like I pretty much slept through the whole thing, but I can't be quite sure? Wow man, how can you have seen all of those mental images but I saw nothing and somehow slept through the whole thing," Wayne puzzled.

I shrugged my shoulders as we walked back inside; it was bitterly cold. (I didn't have the heart to tell Wayne that John had dosed him with the Xanax.) John walked down the hall toward me at a fast pace.

"Okay, Timmy-boy, we have your room ready for you, but just still no TV."

I followed John into Tiffany's old room, which was located just off the living room. It was pretty nice. The bed was neatly made and I could hear the ocean from a cracked window, which made me smile. There was a space heater too, which was awesome since I'd been freezing cold since the treatment.

All of my senses were sharpening. I could hear the slightest tones. In fact, my ears were now ringing intensely from the overuse of my now super-sensitive hearing. While sitting on the bed scanning the room, I noticed a cracked, arched door.

I got off the bed, walked into the small room, and flipped on the light. It was a private bathroom. It had puke-green tile floors and the backsplash was sparkly clean. It had a puke-green tile shower to match. Instantly, I cracked the hot water valve to start warming the water. When walking back into the bedroom, I noticed my bags between the bed and wall, so I quickly shot over, pulled them out and threw them on the bed. I found my wallet in the same side pocket from which Carlo had produced it earlier. Every hundred-dollar-bill was neatly rubber-banded just as the cash had been upon my arrival.

What a fantastic people, I thought. I was astonished; I couldn't even leave valuables of any sort on my desk at work for fear they'd be stolen. Everyone had been so kind and compassionate that I was almost in a state of shock. Even Isabelle and Tiffany who were just patients showed me the most incredible human kindness.

Great cumulus clouds of steam began floating into the bed-room, so I quickly turned my attention to the emergency port on my right hand. The bindings were already about half unwound, but I had far too many distractions since "awaking" to worry about them. Besides, though I felt good, I still wasn't at the top of my game.

I removed the second clip. The first clip was nowhere to be found, and the last one was hanging by a thread. I then re-moved the little bit of medical tape that was keeping the rest of the ace bandage in place. While slowly unwrapping the bandage, I began to think: this little rubber port is my lifeline. If something would've gone wrong, the fellas would've hit me with some adren-aline or something like BOOYAH, I thought.

Just then I noticed the sad, transparent, bent up plastic catheter which rested entirely above the surface of my skin. The *Picc,* which had a tiny drop of my dried blood inside of it, had just fallen to the floor. Experiencing a feeling of helplessness, I went limp. Instantly it occurred to me that if I would've had any trouble at all, they would have shot me with the medication and the medi-cine would have just dribbled all over my arm. The organism would have ceased to be, I thought, as a flashback of God asking me if I wanted to die flashed through my mind. Emitting a great sigh of relief, I took a moment to bask in the epiphany.

15.

The Healing Waters of Tijuana

After Stripping down, butt naked, I walked into the shower and began to adjust the water temperature. The water ran scalding hot, so I tweaked the knobs and decided to pee. It would be the first time I had relieved myself since the waste basket in the dungeon, and I was dreading another bloody investigation.

Suddenly, I experienced an intense burning sensation radiating from my prostate. Upon looking down, I noticed that my penis was shriveled and had the density of a lasso rope. It had constricted so tightly, I'd begun to wonder how urine would even pass through the thing when all of a sudden: "OH FUCK, OH SHIT!" I yelled while experiencing an awful pain in my genitals. The ghastly feeling of my prostate cramping without release was crippling.

At first, I thought something must be miserably wrong with me, but, after considering things, it had also hurt to cry earlier, I thought. Suddenly, it dawned on me; there was no blood in my pee; only a small amount of bright-orange urine trickled from the hole in my now miniaturized penis. That marked the first time in months that my urine wasn't some shade of blood red.

After nearly ten years of being completely numb, I was mutating back into a man. Katie used to say to me, "You don't feel shit. You're just a mindless drone." (Statements like that always made me just want to break down and sob. I thought that there was no way back.)

I would argue with her, saying, "Bullshit. I am the same exact me." (Looking back, I don't think I was anyone, especially in the depths of my problem because I certainly wasn't me anymore.)

Jackpot! The water was perfect, so I hopped in. With eyes closed, I stood in the stream with head bowed and arms crossed while soaking in the heat, which transferred to my body. The water streaming down my body felt very alien, and the manmade Tijuana waterfall instantly transported me to a jungle island. As I stood in the cliff-side waterfall, it reminded me of the label on that expensive island's drinking water. The water seemed to have had some mineral healing quality too, because every cell in my body absorbed the nutrient rich goodness as I came back to life. After drifting a little too far into my thoughts, I opened my eyes as John had recommended, and instantly it all went away; I was back in the Tijuana shower again. (Oh, that is how that was supposed to work!) The trip must have settled into a comfortable level, so the "eyes open trick," which John had recommended, had begun to work. I was still being shown windows to the other side.

Whoa, I respectfully thought. Realizing that the shower experience could last quite a bit longer than I had initially planned, I sat down on the clean puke-green tile. Again with eyes closed, I began hearing the choir of deep monk-like voices echoing: GUU-UUUUUUUUUUM, just as they had at the beginning of my experience and it was comforting as I pondered what was happening.

That GUM noise was the background tone in my head at all times; the sound usually resonated at an inner volume just quieter than my thoughts. I had never noticed the noise before, but I knew it to be something I had lost to the opiates and I felt the strong physical need to join in.

So, there I was lying down in the water stream of the Tijuana-shower chanting "GUUUUUUM" out loud as I reconnected with my experience. The acoustics in the puke-green shower were smashing for that new activity.

Ahhhh, the healing waters of Tijuana, I thought. The shower water felt nice, and continued sheeting over my body like a miraculous rain until, "OH MOTHER FUUUUUCKER – OUCH, OUCH, OUCH." While burning, I jumped out of the shower with haste. My skin shone bright red, and steam rose from of every square inch of me. Now, I both burned and froze at the same time and I could barely see through the thick white cloud that had now formed in the entire bathroom. It was tricky adjusting the hot water valve without burning my arm off as well. With a twist of the knob and a couple of squeaks, the danger was over. Wait a minute. The shower is supposed to run until it eventually turns cold, not hot. *Wasn't it?* I questioned myself. I thought my way through the mechanical possibilities for the stunner and couldn't offer myself an explanation for it.

Fresh clothes never felt so good since I was now so sensitive to the cold. Walking back into the bedroom, I noticed a lot of visual "tracers." When looking up at the ornate glass light globes on the ceiling fan, I saw they were splashing hundreds of the rainbow-colored tracers around the room, reminding me of "electric love." Still famished but not ready for a meal, I thought of some *Tootsie Pops*, which I had stowed in my bags. In my bag I had packed one of those sucker bouquets you see in the stores, and I quickly reached for the orange one.

After unwrapping the candy, I stared at its orange color in wonderment. The orange closely resembled the orange hue that continuously manifested itself in my visions. From the *Tiki* to the orange *juice* (which had coated my brain). The sucker even matched my little orange friend who had now faded almost entirely back into the spirit world. It was the best sucker I had ever had. Never in my life had a flavor made me feel so happy from the inside out. The orange flavor was so intense that it made my mouth pucker and salivate uncontrollably. I gobbled it up and went back out to join Wayne and John, who again sat visiting in the living room.

"Hey guys, what's up?" I asked.

"Nothing. We were just working on some deep shit; what's up with you?" John quizzed as if he were already putting out one emotional fire and wasn't interested in fighting another.

"Oh, nothing. I just thought I'd watch a little TV. Am I bothering the two of you?"

"Oh no, I was just going to bed, but there's no TV. Remember?" John reminded apologetically.

(This was John's cue to bounce, but it didn't bother me.) John went to bed, and it was now just Wayne and me.

"Are you okay, Wayne?" I asked.

"Yeah, dude, again, I am fine. I just feel really weird, almost as if I'm not even myself anymore," Wayne confided.

"Wayne, I'll be completely honest with you. I have no fucking idea what just happened. But I can tell you this: As strange as we may feel now, and I am a bit concerned myself, I was so damned sick before, man. I am living minute by minute too, Wayne, but I must admit that I'm already so much better than where I was at before."

"Oh yeah, you're so right; I don't disagree with you about that. I'm just so mind-blown right now. I'm trying to wrap my head around all of it; you know?"

Even in my treatment psychosis, I realized how crucial the "visions" were to the experience. My psychedelic bunkmate went through the same things as I did, save for the imagery, and he was "healed" yet still very confused. And as otherworldly as the things I'd witnessed were, I realized that the visions were the key to understanding the entire process. But, what was the difference? I wondered.

Why would the visions give me peace and Wayne's lack of visions leave him feeling so empty and confused? I had some experience with *entheogens* in the past but how could that experience have been so fundamentally and profoundly different from all of the other times? For example: When I'd done LSD or mushrooms in the past I'd had some revelations and profound enlightenment but, just before the breakthrough thoughts revealed their final conclusions, they just vanished. Afterward, I was left feeling like an absolute moron for ever placing stock in those thoughts at all.

The Ibogaine experience seemed to make more sense as time went on. The Iboga hallucinations seemed to have an even deeper meaning as I continued to think about them. What's more, I still remembered most of the visual portion of the experience. In fact, I would recall more of the content as time passed rather than having it slip through my fingers as it had done during all of those other times.

Most of those prior experiences weren't even all that profound in comparison, mainly walls breathing, some mental special effects, and an extraordinary interest in patterns. I am not saying those experiences weren't crazy intense or mind numbing, but the intellectual content was very abstract, to say the least.

All of the other hallucinogenic experiences were just explainable madness by trips' end; that is it then, I thought to myself. Maybe the long Ibogaine trip just wasn't finished yet, and I was still just tripping. Wayne and I continued our conversation for hours.

I discovered throughout the night, though Wayne didn't experience what I had, unlike the other fellas, he had had an unnatural attention span for what I had to say about it. Wayne was in the same zone, so to speak. I felt it was helpful for Wayne to have heard my experience for understanding what had happened to him. Wayne and I discussed earthly and cosmic mysteries until around 2:00 am. Still, I don't think either one of us were very sleepy in a physical sense. All the same, even the magical afterglow of Ibogaine couldn't keep us from our presupposed necessity for sleep. So, with the optimism of a toddler, I moved to my room.

After tucking myself in, my stomach began to feel as if it were eating itself. Stomach pangs now felt like someone was driving a wooden stake into my gut. I yelled for Carlo and whined about being hungry except "nothing sounded good." I reminded myself of a whiney mate whose ego was only seeking attention, but I was in so much pain. I had turned into a psychiatrist psychoanalyzing my exaggerated self-serving behavior from the outside. Analyzing the situation, I recognized myself as selfish but rationalized myself as a paying consumer. And, though being 2:00 am, I consciously continued the deviant behavior. In real time I saw flaws in myself as they'd occurred. Observations the way others see me were being made instead of my viewing myself in the usual biased-sense.

Carlo arrived and ran through a myriad of snack choices until he finally got to "oatmeal." "Would you mind heavily cutting it with milk so I can drink it, Carlo?" I helplessly requested. (My stomach was *jacked* up.)

"I will blend it for you, Mr. Tim."

I felt like an absolute douche-nozzle. I consciously realized I was acting self-serving and then allowed Carlo to cater to that selfish behavior, and it concerned me until he re-visited me with the beloved concoction.

"Thank you, Carlo. I am so sorry for waking you; go back to bed. I am good now."

I drank the thick, delectable liquid-treat and the warm feeling of content forced me to sleep.

16.

Jungle TV

Like a resurrected human being, I awoke and reported to the vacant living room. My lonely morning was devoted to a quiet black TV, after fog denied me an ocean view. Still, happiness overjoyed me. The DVD player clock caught my attention just as it flipped from 7:59 to 8:00 am. The workers once more poured into the beach house. Unprovoked smiles made me happy, and my outlook on life was active and fresh.

"Would you like that smoothie now?" Chef again asked with the same charades-like Spanglish dialect.

We both laughed as the workers didn't scatter but instead surrounded Chef and me.

Each member of the group individually wore a smile as they all gazed at us cheerfully. They giggled and visited among themselves, continuously pointing and making observations. Speaking quickly in Spanish, the tempo and volume of the chatter grew as they all competed to talk at once. They were intrigued by my 180-degree change in demeanor. My smile must have been shiny also because they were hypnotized by me that morning.

After a bit, the group dismantled and quickly tackled their household duties. Just as had happened before, doors, hatches, and cabinets slammed in the eager group's wake; Chef handed me my smoothie. The sound of the front door opening and shutting again had caught my attention as John came strolling in again, holding his gym bag, "How are you feeling today, Timmy?" John inquired as he walked down the hall toward us.

"I'm feeling awesome, John. My nerves are a little sketchy. I feel like running a marathon or something but, wow…overall I feel fantastic."

"You actually bounced back quickly, Timmy," John said while giving me a visual once-over. "Don't worry about that nervous feeling, either; that's called *motivation* and is normal but will likely take a little while for you to become accustomed. It will likely take your brain some time to get used to almost everything without the sedating effects of the medicine."

"I'm so happy, what a miracle," I acknowledged.

Grady came walking up from the dungeon and asked, "What's up, dudes?"

Grady was entering my personal space and had a mean, I TOLD YOU SO, look on his face. When Grady came mere inches from me, he growled, "TOLD YOU SO MOTHERFUCKER, TOLD YOU SO! YOU ARE NOW IN THE BROTHERHOOD, BITCH! YOU LOOK GORGEOUS; CLEANLINESS LOOKS GOOD ON YOU, TIMMY!"

Grady continued celebrating as his mean-mugging faded into a kind smile and a bear hug. He finished with a series of excruciating high fives resulting in a bright red throbbing hand. It was a relief to see Wayne stepping out of his room. He was in his jammies, was chipper, and looked great too.

"Good morning, Wayne," we altogether agreed.

We shared an incredible sense of community, hope, and freedom. That stretch of coastal Mexico was very intriguing to me, too, so I couldn't wait to see what the day held through bright eyes.

"What do you guys want to do today?" Grady questioned.

"What do people usually do after you and your partner, John, are done turning your spiritual tricks?" Wayne asked.

"Well, usually, we have Hayden take the group down to a resort called, *Las Rocas*, near Ensenada. Fishing is pretty popular too among a lot of the patients. They usually enjoy the sauna, massages, swimming, and all that shit," Grady said as he finished selling the package to us.

"That sounds awesome," Wayne and I agreed.

"We would take you guys for hookers, but the guys a couple of groups ahead of you ruined that for the rest," Grady said disappointedly. We broke out into laughter.

"That's okay, Grady, I'm good on hookers," I said as Wayne showed agreement by way of a quick, exaggerated head-nod.

Grady continued, "The same group ruined a lot of shit for everyone. God, they were fucking crazy. Unbeknownst to us… The one guy had packed a grip of smack in his bag and, when treatment was over, he decided to share. Several of them took him up on the offer, and it was an absolute mess. I just sent them all home and kept their money, fuckers."

He continued, "It was never my intention to run this place like a jailhouse but when guys like that ruin other peoples' chances of recovery; it's where I have to draw the line. So, that same group is also why you boys got the shakedown when you arrived," Grady finished.

"Hey, Grady, at some point, I would like to hit up a dentist to rework some old fillings while I'm here. Do either of you know of a good one?"

"Seriously, you want to go to the dentist while you're here in Tijuana, Timmy?" Grady puzzled.

"I'm a big boy, Grady. Don't you know anyone good?" I now begged.

"Okay, I will ask Silva where you should go. But, if it totally fucking sucks, I told you so, motherfucker. Trust me when I say this: It ain't the same here, Timmy," Grady again sternly warned.

"How did you boys sleep last night?" John rejoined the conversation.

"I slept like a champ," Wayne confirmed.

"Yeah, same, I didn't get to bed till late. I watched quite a deal of TV before falling asleep. But, once I did, I slept solidly for like four hours," I finished informing the group.

"What did you watch on 'TV' last night, Timmy?" Grady asked with a snicker.

"The news, which is crazy here. There were a lot of in-fomercials too. Mostly the dumb slow-mo drug commercials, but there were a lot of screaming pitchmen as well," I replied. The whole group now looked on with great-big smiles on their faces. "What?" I asked while scanning the happy faces within the group.

"We don't have TV," Grady said as the entire group erupted.

Oh, my God, Grady is right, I thought.

"What the fuck?" I asked.

"Tim was watching the *Forest Television* last night," John said as the group indulged in a second heaping helping of laughter.

"What is, 'forest television,' John?" I asked as the group continued laughing at me hysterically.

"That's what the natives of the Peruvian Amazon call *Ayahuasca*, which is the longer-lasting, ingestible form of DMT, which you guys smoked the other night," John schooled.

"Very amusing. Hey, I have a good idea. You guys should add *Jungle TV* to that long list of other shit on your website that you don't really have."

"About all of that, I'm sorry we don't have the amenities that we listed on our website," Grady said.

"Yeah, what's up with that?" Wayne asked.

"Yeah, this place doesn't even match the pictures on your website. I'm pretty sure that this house changed colors while I was tripping, too," I added.

"Well, we weren't gonna tell you boys any of this, but, I guess telling you now won't hurt anything. Timmy, you're right. We did have the house painted while you were out. I know this is all very confusing, guys. Okay, well, I guess I'll just start from the top," Grady spoke with great seriousness as the group hushed.

"Four days ago, we were operating out of our own actual hospital, and it was in fact located in Rosarito, just as we advertise on our website. It's actually where *Coretta Scott King* died, back in 2004. We were renting the place. Coretta is *Martin Luther King*'s widow. It was a fantastic location and facility, and we were just about to ramp things up to an epic scale.

"While conducting our usual business that day, dozens of Mexican Marinos armed with automatic rifles surrounded and stormed our facility. With guns drawn they began to move everything in the hospital out into the parking lot—including the patients," Grady finished.

"Oh, my God, Grady! Were the patients tripping at the time, like I was?" I asked.

"Um, you could say that. We'd just given several patients their flood doses, immediately after which big, armed Mexican Marines surrounded the patients at gunpoint. The Marinos wheeled them into the parking lot, one-by-one, while still in their beds. John was going crazy. He even had his shirt off like a red-neck, taking part in a bar throw down. And, I can say, *redneck,* because I'm an Irish-American, Mexican, Texas redneck."

He continued, "John was screaming at the Marines as they continued to sweep the entire facility clean of us, our shit, and our patients. I felt so bad for the patients because I can't imagine how the scene looked to them right after their flood doses. There was nothing we could do about it; we just ensured our patients' safety as our priority, and then I rented this beach house. We all busted our asses to make this a seamless transition for you guys. It's actu-ally a funny story.

"We sent Chef into the house right ahead of your arrival, with only a sack of groceries and some pans, and told him to make some noise and make it sizzle. I called another Ibogaine clinic, which John and I had helped start-up before we started this place. Thankfully, they were happy to take our patients, as long as we paid them what the patients had paid us for the treatment. Tiffany and Isabelle were the only two we could bring with us.

"Tiffany was gonna be here till her mom got tired of paying us and Isabelle had already paid for two weeks in advance, so we'd already treated her the week prior. Tiffany's mom snapped yester-day and finally wanted her home.

"Everyone here in Mexico is on the take. I guess that the racket is probably also why they stormed our hospital in the first place. The rent was all paid up for six months, but, I suppose someone in the mix didn't get their cut," Grady proudly finished.

"That is insane, Grady," Wayne remarked with his mouth agape.

"Thank God they didn't say all of that ahead of time," Wayne whispered.

"Wow, Grady! Are things really that crooked around here?" I asked in disbelief.

"Timmy, you're in Mexico, Homie. If the policia pull you over for anything at all, you can pay them off and just drive off like nothing happened."

"How much would that cost, for example, Grady?" I questioned.

"For speeding, Timmy? Twenty bucks can get you out of almost anything at all, barring a murder or something, I suppose. Even then, you could probably do the same if you had access to four or five-hundred bucks," Grady finished with a chuckle.

"Hmmm, can I drive the rental car to Rosarito?" I asked.

"Are you gonna try and get a speeding ticket?" Grady asked.

"Fuck, yes! I've heard of this before in Rocky Point, Mexico. Do you mind?"

"Fuck it; I got the extra insurance, so go for it. Not today, though. If you're still up to it in a day, or so, after the mania dies down, I don't mind," Grady agreed.

"I am not kidding, Grady."

"I'm not either, fool," Grady assured in a deep voice with a huge smile.

It seemed all of those cats had lost their addictions but not that tight drug-buddy fellowship. Undoubtedly, that same sense of camaraderie lured us into that lifestyle, to begin with. We all filled a void where something was missing.

I changed the subject. "Hey, Grady. You guys need to change the sheets in my room because there's sand or something in them. Maybe they forgot to change them after Tiffany left?"

"No, dude, I am pretty sure they were all changed, but I will have the crew change them again if you like, Timmy."

"Please, Grady? Thank you. I'd like that."

The ocean once again garnered my attention through those large glass windows since the fog had now burned off, and it matched the sky's gorgeous shades of blue. As I walked out through the still permanently stuck-open glass sliding door, the Pacific's great beauty consumed me whole. Instinctively I raised my arms toward the sky in a form of universal thanksgiving, and another whale and her calf breached the ocean's surface. It was cold, and I experienced the densest groupings of goosebumps.

Looking back up at the horizon, I had the unique perspective of floating in midair on a giant water-covered rock; for the first time, I perceived our Earth in its macrocosm. Earth no longer felt like the center of our universe, nor did I have the sensation of being "grounded" while standing on Earth and I was humbled completely. After being rendered completely inert by the sheer mass of the universe, I tightened my scarf and walked back inside with a great sense of appreciation.

Carlo was lugging five-gallon jugs of purified water into the house and carrying them into the pantry.

"We all appreciate your effort in the prevention of Montezuma's revenge, Carlo," Wayne said with a big grin.

"Oh, my God."

The proverbial phrase… "Don't drink the water," echoed loudly in my head. While picturing green, microscopic single-celled gyrating monsters, I remembered brushing my teeth with the funky liquid.

"Oh, fuck, guys. I've been brushing my teeth with that shit since the moment I arrived," I whined.

"Quit tripping, Timmy. That's mostly blown out of proportion," John assured.

"No fucking way, dude. I've been coming here for decades, and I wouldn't drink that shit," Wayne interjected.

"Fuck it. I'll drink a glass of TJ tap water right now just to prove it to you naysayers," John announced.

"Come-on, that shit is wack as fuck, bro! John, please don't do it. I need you, Son," Grady pleaded.

Chef quickly gathered the non-English speakers while muttering in Spanish as they too joined the crowd in disbelief. John grabbed a large, clean glass out from the clean dish rack and filled it to the brim straight from the kitchen tap. Before anyone could begin to talk him out of the stunt, John tipped the glass and with five or six giant successive gulps, he chugged the whole thing. John slammed the glass on the counter and with a couple of jaw exercises, thrust a long deep belch upon the astonished crowd who stood quietly in disbelief. John exploded with laughter.

"You're all a bunch of pussies," John shouted as he continued the laughing spell.

With mouths open in astonishment, the expressions on the faces in the crowd remained unchanged. John may as well have transformed that glass of Tijuana tap water into wine.

With the miracle's end, Grady said, "Hey, Timmy, check your sheets now and see if they feel better."

I removed my shirt on the short walk to my room, and while almost shivering, I settled into a fetal position to conserve body warmth. When performing an investigative body roll, the sheets were abrasive to my arms and chest but not my face or back. What the heck, how is that possible? I disbelieved. Studying my right arm intently, I still saw with such clarity. I wondered if my corrected astigmatism had lasted beyond the experience because the hairs on my arm seemed magnified.

A quick finger to and fro, along the top of my arm hairs made me realize that it was not sand at all; the sheets were perfectly clean. The "sand feeling" was emanating from the hairs on my own body. My senses had become so completely numb by the medicine that my very body hair had become alien to me.

"Thank you, Grady," I shouted from my room while keeping my discovery a secret.

After a brief pause, I heard the faint, "You're welcome, Timmy."

17.

No Anesthetic

After the sand in the bed incident, I walked back out to the kitchen and rejoined the group.

"Get ready, Timmy. You and Wayne are going to Las Rocas today," Grady said.

"Is that the resort you were telling us about?" Wayne asked.

"Yeah man, spa day, boys; you're going to love it. Get in the sauna and clean the rest of those funky ass toxins out of your body," Grady continued selling us on the package.

"Geez, if you want us gone just say it, Grady," Wayne quipped with a grin.

"John and I were just discussing what a chill group you and Timmy are."

"Well, sorry we didn't bring a little heroin to spice things up around here," Wayne joked with the two.

(We all got a quite a laugh.)

Hayden (Mr. Business-Party-hairdo) drove Wayne and me back down the coast, past where Grady and I had gone to *Wal-Mart* the evening prior until a giant, 75-foot open-armed Jesus greeted us from high on a hilltop. The Jesus statue was a lot like the one in Rio De Janeiro, Brazil, except the Mexican one was painted and stood atop a dome. *Jesus* was on a hilltop mixed in with a scattering of mansions that were all gleaming at the mighty Pacific. Our Lord gracefully gazed over the top of a large, sprawling white adobe-style complex, which also faced the Pacific.

The hotel complex stood on a tall bluff over-guarding a crescent-shaped cove; the entire coast was very rocky. Hayden walked Wayne and me into the spa, which was up tall outdoor stairs. A commercial aluminum-framed glass door sealed the entrance to the establishment. Hayden had the money situation squared away, and Wayne and I headed into the spa area, which was magnificent; the resort opened right up to the ocean. Large, glass plates framed the vast blue sea beautifully.

The top level of the spa where we stood must have been a hundred feet in elevation above the sea. Great ships and small sailboats crept along in the foamy salt water in all directions. The vessels, which didn't seem to move at all, left tiny white lines behind them, scarring the ocean's surface. The view left me feeling insignificant and like a God at once. I tried to sit in the sauna for a while but couldn't for long since it was hot, and my organism was far too sensitive. While Wayne and I sat in the sauna, two guys sitting directly across from Wayne and me were discussing their Ibogaine trips. After some small talk, we informed them that we too were in Mexico for Ibogaine treatment, and it turned out they were just from a different clinic. They also seemed to be in high spirits. The realization that this wackiness was all just an acceptable modality of treatment in Mexico had only begun to set in.

From what I saw, Mexican medicine was far more transparent than medicine in the US. They were clearly not as well-equipped technology-wise but were light years ahead of us in forward thinking. Wayne explained, "The Mexican medical culture is strewn with natural remedies that have been around for hundreds, if not thousands, of years."

"Wayne, I see that, but I'm just having a hard time with this. How can this be illegal in the States? It's blowing my mind."

"Here, I'll blow your mind, Timmy. LSD is the cure for alcoholism, and the government has known it since the sixties. They banned LSD not long after a doctor in Canada was documenting amazing results in a clinical experiment. His results showed a 53% higher success rate with LSD than traditional psychotherapy which I think is around 12% successful. Something like that."

"Alcohol kills more people than painkillers, and they advertise booze right next to Doritos during the Super Bowl. America is a free country, as long as you're the right color, and you share the same taste and religious beliefs as the hypocrites in Washington."

"C'mon, Wayne, that's bullshit, right?"

"Sorry, Timmy, not bullshit. Look it up for yourself. Our government has to change. Bill Wilson, the co-founder of Alcoholics Anonymous cured his alcoholism with a hallucinogenic called Belladonna in the early 1900s. That cure was on the front page of the New York Times in 1909, but too was quickly demonized and forgotten about.

"We have to get lobbyists out of Washington before they kill us all with that shit. Same with Ibogaine. No one would ever abuse that shit, Timmy, but it hit DEA's schedule I chart immediately after a heroin addict tried Ibogaine and realized that he no longer wished to use heroin. The minute he patented it, as a true miracle addiction drug, it became illegal with no research whatsoever.

"We have to get control over our ignorance, man. The first arrests ever for Ibogaine happened to be a couple in Wyoming who were trying to kick their Hydrocodone habit in 2005. They are among the only few arrests for the drug that I am even aware of, ever. So, can Ibogaine truly be severely addictive with a high probability of abuse, as the DEA's bullshit *Schedule I chart* advertises? Law enforcement threw them both in jail for trying to cure their addiction, for the same thing we just did.

"The government should NOT be able to tell lies about drugs, legal *or illegal*; it's all the same.

"Lies about things like drugs are dangerous, deadly dangerous. They almost got us, too, Timmy. Meanwhile, drugs like marijuana are Schedule I and have never harmed a soul. How many people wouldn't touch a pill if their pot was legal? And, every son-of-a-bitch is hooked on benzos like Xanax.

"You can die if you try quitting Xanax, or similar drugs, cold-turkey, and they sell them on TV stateside. That drug is so dangerous, Timmy. That, you can die from, if you *stop* taking it. Look at Sarah; she kicked the worst heroin habit I've ever heard of and is still weaning herself off of the Xanax, and they hand that shit out like candy in the states."

Wayne continued, "What are we thinking? My dad opened my eyes to all of this shit. Remember? He was a surgeon who died of an OD as an old man, from the same string of lies.

"I hate to be the one to break this to you, Timmy, but the painless, all natural, overnight cure to addiction is illegal in the states, punishable by twenty years in a cage. Do the math, son; legal drug dealing is all it is, right? You can take all the drugs you want, mix and match. Fuck, go kill yourself if you like, Timmy, as long as you get your drugs from Uncle Sam.

"We've made illegal the cures to addictions and disorders, son. The US government is more ruthless than El Chappo. That's why they want to find him and bring him back to the US; they want to thin the competition."

With that, Wayne and I were each called into small, dark, private rooms.

My masseuse was a small, robust, Mexican girl who appeared to be native to the Oaxaca region. She started on my left foot, and the sensation was also quite alien (like the sand in my bed). It felt good, but, mostly like extreme pain. There was nothing sexual at all about the massage, but I began to become aroused anyhow. Attempting every mental trick I knew, I tried not to become erect, but, the more I tried, the more erect I became.

Within seconds, I was rock hard, so I peeked under the rag on my face to inspect the event, which was highly visible, even from underneath the blanket. Discretely, I used my right hand to readjust, but again, it was no use. I could now see my penis throbbing through the blanket. As soon as the little masseuse worked her way up to my left calf, I could feel the beginnings of an orgasm.

Right away, it was evident that all of the mental "grandma, grandma, grandma" exercises in the world wouldn't stop the subsequent event. I quickly cupped my hand over the end, so not to make a mess, and I could already feel the warm sensation of ejaculation in my hand. And it hurt, *horribly*. Thankfully, I wasn't even focusing on the excruciating pain since it was so awkward.

Ashamed now, and with all of that hot slimy shit in my hand, I thought: Hopefully she didn't see that, but it seemed she had because she stopped working on my left calf, quickly gave my right calf a couple of courtesy pumps and hastily worked her way around to my right hand. My God! I squeezed my eyes shut tight while bracing for the most embarrassing moment of my life. I rolled my hand under the blanket so she'd forget it even existed in the first place. WELL, SHE DIDN'T FORGET.

The young señorita grabbed my clenched fist and pulled it out from underneath the blanket after which she forced my hand open. My whole body went completely limp as I felt her tiny plump hand begin to open mine. Here we go, I thought. Uneventfully, she kindly wiped my DNA from the hand with a warm wet rag. (She had witnessed that whole pathetic show and drew no unwanted attention to the situation. Two words: human compassion.)

Throughout the week there were many more trips to "Las Rocas." It's not what you think – thank God. No visit was as eventful or embarrassing as that. Each massage made my body more tolerant of the environment. The señorita spoke no English, either – none – not even "hello, " so there was never an awkward, inappropriate or revisited moment. I kept my happy-ending moment a secret from the fellas.

Believe it or not, that moment changed something in me in a good way: Somehow that one beautiful person's caring action set me free from criticism of self by self and by others. Or perhaps, the Ibogaine did, and the event only poured the emotional slag from the top of my new soul after its casting. In either event, from that moment forward I've enjoyed a taste of Nathan's freedom of shamelessness since Ibogaine tore my social walls of disguise down in that great spiritual finale.

Well, not as shameless as Nathan – I'm still working on that – what a blessing. (I can't help but wonder: Maybe, Nathan treated his emotional trauma long ago in that fateful Dallas nightclub, The Starck Club.)

On another such Las Rocas visit, Hayden dropped me off, as usual. Wayne didn't come, so I was left there alone. (It was unbelievable to me that "Ibogaine University" didn't trust me to "leave the compound" only a few days ago when I was a drug addict and now I was free to move around the country.)

I had brought a hundred dollars and Grady had lent me a clam-shell style "burner phone" that I had thought about calling Katie on but had quickly realized the battery was nearly dead. After my massage, I took a needed shower and asked the girl womaning the front desk to phone me a cab. A tall, clean-cut Mexican boy in his twenties pulled up in an old black two-door Civic with a Hand-shaker tranny and the Arm-strong window package. (If you're not one, that's car-guy for a manual transmission and manual roll-up windows.) Ramon's Civic also had several primer gray splotches.

To my surprise, "Ramon" spoke some English, so I explained where I was going. It seemed simple to me since IU was right on the ocean, directly across from the "Colegio de La Frontera Norte." We drove through an obscure mountain pass that opened up to piles of small stucco houses with clotheslines attached to all of them. Ramon explained that the neighborhood, which stretched to the horizon, was a "squatter hood."

After seeing the visions, I no longer looked at the houses as hovels; they were just homes, with people living in them.

Right away, after realizing we were lost, I opened up the cell phone and dialed the *Grady* contact in the phonebook. The

Page 237

call went right to voicemail, and the "battery icon" on the cell-phone began blinking rapidly. Immediately, I felt a ridiculous white-knuckle diarrhea cramp.

Oh God... Go figure, I thought. John drank a tall glass of Tijuana tap-water and was fine, but for some crazy reason, I brushed my teeth with it only few times, and now it seems that I am now going to shit allover myself? I thought to myself. *Really?*

The trip had taken a quick right turn for the worst.

Awe fuck, Ramon, I have to shit Now! Ramon no longer understood *ANY* English. "Que?" he kept asking me. I mentally arranged the words in Spanish and then realized my crappy dialect with a shout,"NECESITO EL SHITTER AHORA. BAÑOS, BAÑOS, RAMON," I begged.

"Si Señor," Ramon said as he smashed the gas pedal to the floor mat. There were zero restrooms there.

Finally, several intimidating, sun-darkened men with giant mustaches and furrowed faces, stood around an old auto-repair shop. The whole place, even the parking lot had been carved into the mountain pass that we had just flipped-bitch to exit.

We pulled in right next to the crowd, which was oriented to my side of the car and Ramon ducked to make eye contact with the "Caballeros" through my window as I leaned back. A heavy draft of air which bore the odor of cigarettes and fresh gasoline was present—*even though none of them were smoking or pouring gas.* A quick exchange of some highly respectful Spanish dialogue took place, and the men pointed at a door near the rear of a white-brick building; I sprinted to the spot. Never before or since have I been so happy to see a dirty restroom with no toilet paper.

The fact remained, however, that after the spackling had taken place, there was still no toilet paper. A glance down at my socks, which are my usual go-to remedy when hunting, turned up NO SOCKS, DAMNIT. I ripped the right sleeve from my t-shirt and carefully got to work. With such limited resources, there was no margin for error.

Almost there, I thought, as I frantically ripped off the other sleeve. On the way back to Ramon's car, I enjoyed a great sigh of relief while looking a whole lot like *Larry the Cable Guy*.

My entire body seemed to be righting itself, and there were surprises around every corner.

When Ramon drove us from the final mountain pass, I again powered-on the phone and tried Grady, who answered while the battery icon blinked erratically. When Grady picked-up, I tossed the phone to Ramon like a red-hot nickel and the two spoke Spanish for just a few seconds until the phone died. "I think I know now," Ramon confirmed. We raced up the freeway as our star disappeared into the horizon. Finally, a moonlit college and the billboard of Donald Trump came into view, and I have never been so happy to see his haystack.

The following night, I slept more than six hours and woke up refreshed. (I'm pretty sure that was the first time I'd even slept since arriving in Mexico.)

Silva had already made my dentist appointment with a trusted friend and colleague, and Carlo and I headed to his office first thing the next morning.

Tijuana was crazy. We passed zebras in the streets, a Jai-Alai arena, which reminded me of the beginning of the show *Miami Vice*, and an arch that looked like the one in Saint Louis, Missouri. Carlo pointed proudly at the structure and began a tour of grunts that were slowly deciphered to, "That's just like the one you have in the USA. Ours wasn't supposed to have all of those wires on it, though. The day it opened, the wind was blowing so hard they thought it was going to fall.

"They then added all of those cables to it," Carlo proudly finished. Upon closer inspection, wires threaded the inside of the arch like bicycle spokes and that, for some reason, made me giggle.

"Are you really up for this?" Carlo asked as we approached the front door of the clinic, in the heart of Tijuana.

"Of course, Carlo. Why does everyone keep asking me that?"

"Crazy gringo," Carlo shook his head with a grin.

I'm pretty sure he was the best dentist in all of TJ since all of TJ was there in his little waiting room. When I walked in with Carlo, you would've thought I was from another planet. Carlo asked me if I wanted to go right to the front of the waiting list, to which I replied, "FUCK, YES."

"Give me ten bucks then," Carlo demanded.

He handed the lovely Mexican girl my sawbuck to which she said with a smile, "Follow me." We walked straight back to the dentist chair, and I took a seat. The dentist and I shared a little small talk, and he got right down to business.

"What do you hope to accomplish today?" the dentist asked in succinct English.

"Well, I haven't been to the dentist for about four years. Three fillings seem to be wearing a little thin. They are twenty-four years old. I also wanna do X-rays and have a cleaning while I'm here," I opened my mouth as directed.

"Ah yes, I see… All three are leaking. Well, we can do the two fillings to maximize your trip, and you can get the single one on the other side redone in the states if you want? I know you

Page 240

gringos like to have your faces numb. Or, I can just work without anesthetic like the locals. I can do them all at once, then," the dentist offered.

"Um, some people have their teeth drilled with no anesthetic?" I asked in horror.

"'Some people,' Tim? More like, everyone in Mexico."

"That's loco, doc."

"Numbing your face, or anything else for that matter, is something that we take very seriously in Mexico. We won't even do it unless you're having an invasive procedure such as a root canal. I cannot numb both sides of your face at once anyway; you will likely chew your tongue off.

"Americans usually ask for the X-ray films also, Tim, but I'm afraid those aren't necessary either. I will charge you for them if you still want," he quipped condescendingly with a laugh.

"What? Why?" I asked.

"Well, to tell the truth, unless there's pain that I cannot visually see the cause of, the films are also unnecessary. Think about it, Tim. Cavities form from the outside of the enamel, not the inside. And, once the decay is severe enough to drill, the tooth enamel is already destroyed, right? We're just going to bore the wall of the tooth out. So, why not just drill it out and repair it then? The US has brainwashed the American public into thinking that dental X-rays are a necessary precaution, and that does two things. "

He continued, "One—it allows the provider to overcharge you grossly for the films.

"And two—it's the perfect opportunity to update your FBI profile so that they can keep track of you in your 'free country.'"

"And, there is always a chance that the radiation will catch your cells dividing and give you cancer. If you gringos had *our* freedom and *your* resources, you would have a utopia. Aye, yai, yai, what a waste. Hey, just lay your hand flat on your chest and if the drilling begins to hurt, simply raise it up, and I will stop."

Without another word, I placed my hand on my chest, and the dentist's drilling began. Out of instinct alone, I raised my hand instantly, and the drilling ceased. (It was a SHOCK.)

"Sensitivity is never pain, Tim. It may be shocking, but don't mistake it as pain, okay?" he requested as a full latex glove flashed an OK sign in my periphery.

(From his change of tone alone, I could feel some respect from the dentist for giving their culture a little test spin; the sarcasm was put on hold.) He resumed work with his miniature power tools. Though stiff, my hand never raised again. The dentist raised a mirror to show me my hollowed-out teeth, and I was flabbergasted.

"All done with the good part," the dentist remarked.

(Okay, the sarcasm was already back, but I could still feel my human level, cultural exchange, street-credit strengthening.) With a few squirts of filler, I was closing my mouth to check the bite.

"Now bite down," the dentist would say after each tooth.

A couple of my teeth didn't fit just-so, and, therefore, required modification with a mini-power sander. "See, Timoteo, if your face were numb, how could you tell me the filling is too high?

"Aye, pinche gringos," he quietly grumbled.

(That was true, I could remember my jaw not working right after I got those three fillings, all in the same day, at the age of 16.

Also, the cancer and FBI stuff may or may not have been true, but the good dentist was certainly right about another thing: it was intense, but never hurt.) The dental assistant, who was the dentist's 14-year-old son, raised the mirror back to my face and from my reflection, I could see that all of my silver fillings were now white; I couldn't even tell where the old fillings once were. We all shared a couple more laughs, and then things got right down to business. "How much do I owe you, Doc," I asked as if I were in an *Old Western* movie? (I couldn't resist.)

"Let's see," he wondered, staring into space while running figures using some super-accurate mid-air finger-pointing technique.

"That will be eighty-five dollars and fifty-eight cents, please," the doc kindly stated.

"Seriously?" I perked up.

"Well, let's see here, again," the dentist scrambled.

"It was just the three fillings, and... plus the cleaning... We did a lot of work," the dentist rationalized, as he double checked his finger-pointing.

I gladly handed the good dentist two-hundred dollars American, interrupting his dramatic collection routine. (I also gave his assistant a twenty, and you would have thought I had paid off both of their mortgages.)

There was lots of appreciation shown by all three parties, including myself. Walking out, I felt like John Wayne. I didn't even need a shot of tequila, I thought, as I chuckled loudly; I cannot begin to explain how invincible I felt. As long as this feeling holds up, I will have now accomplished everything that I came to Mexico for, I thought. (I couldn't help but still be a little skeptical that this Ibogaine thing might be temporary but only time would tell.)

On the way home, we stopped at a pharmacy so I could buy cigarettes and I noticed how inexpensive the OTC medications were. Most antibiotics, muscle relaxers, etcetera, that were pre-scription-only in the US, were all Over-The-Counter, in Mexico. My OTC stomach medicine only cost a tiny fraction of what I gave for it in the States, and I received ten-times as many tablets.

Carlo drove me to the bank. He recommended that I change my hundreds for twenty dollar bills, after explaining, "That's a lot of money here, so all those hundreds could get you robbed, Tim."

We wound up driving to three separate banks to change all of the hundred-dollar notes into twenties.

When we arrived back at the beach house (me still looking like *Larry the Cable Guy*), the real Mexican cable guy was just finishing with the TV and internet connections. A quick jostle through my bags produced my laptop, and after frantically keying-in the password for the WIFI, I ran to my room and began to Face-Time Katie.

"Hi honey, you look great. Oh, my God, your eyes are so clear and shiny," Katie said. "Ha - ha - ha, nice shirt!" Katie sar-castically noted.

"Don't ask," I replied.

Smiling big, I gazed at her beautiful dark-blue eyes.

"Thank you so much, baby. I feel right again," I replied as a tear rolled down my cheek and turned to a laugh as I made the statement. (Again, I laughed because I couldn't believe that I felt good and could *feel* again at all.)

"Hey Katie, I just found out that Wayne is leaving on Friday. His wife is coming to get him so I'll just catch a ride with him back to the border. I'll find my way to the airport from there instead of coming home on Sunday. What do you think?" I finished.

"Oh, that sounds great, Tim."

Just then, a rapping could be heard on my bedroom door. The door cracked, and three smiley faces could be seen peeking through it – Carlo, Nurse Jessica, and Hayden.

"You cannot go until Sunday, as promised," Carlo said.

"Why Carlo? Wayne is leaving then."

"I don't know, Tim. That's just what Mr. John said, you cannot go."

Jessica looked very disappointed in me for trying to escape.

"Okay, that is fine. Can I talk to Katie now?"

"I guess," Carlo said, as he shut the door behind them.

After turning my attention back to Katie on my computer screen, my frown melted back into a smile.

"Oh well, it was worth a try, right?" Katie asked.

That was the final piece of the puzzle; I could tell that Katie still loved me.

"It's okay, Babe—I understand—I am so happy for you. No, I am glad for *us!* You just enjoy the rest of your stay there, and I will be here when you get back, okay?"

That was all I'd needed; I could just relax and enjoy the rest of my week now, I thought.

"Happy Valentine's Day, Baby!" Katie happily remarked. "Oh, I almost forgot. Go in the garage; look in the cabinet where I keep my tools."

Katie walked into the garage and grabbed a stuffed animal, a heart-shaped box of chocolates, and a card.

"Oh honey, I can't believe you remembered me," she marveled.

"I wouldn't have forgotten you for the world; I love you so dearly. I'm sorry you have to put up with all of my bullshit."

The prophetic personal note inside read, "My dear Katie, I thought that I would give you and the girls the very best Valentine's Day gift of all – getting clean. I love you and the girls more than life itself. We will be together very soon. (CLEAN THIS TIME.) Tim"

Throughout that week, there was a lot of rest. Wayne and I formed a bond that will last the rest of our lives; we had become brothers in every sense of the word. We smoked cig after cig on his private back-porch, which overlooked the Pacific Ocean. We whale-watched and shared things that I have never shared with another single soul. Our strange circumstances seemed to give us permission to talk about anything in the world.

Now-and-then, Wayne and I heard the intermittent muting of an outboard motor bouncing beneath the wake. We sat and smoked from Wayne's incredible view, high above the ocean and islands and watched the occasional jet-ski or motor-boat with a stuck-open throttle, head for the "invisible line in the water." Sometimes there was a chase vehicle and sometimes not but they always ran wide-open. Wayne and I, both got quite a kick out of the bravery of the outlaws.

18.

Ticker Tape Parade

So, there you have it. Believe it or not, I got clean overnight, in a basement near Tijuana, Mexico, through the use of a psychedelic root bark that grows at the base of a shrub from Gabon Africa; a rite of passage for the Bwiti tribe.

There were visions of biblical magnitude that all had to do with my life in one way or the other, and, as time moved forward, instead of them going away, they had become more pronounced, solidifying the lessons that they had taught me.

The balance of the single week in Mexico I spent in resorts getting massages, doing yoga, getting my teeth drilled with no anesthetic, and just tooling around the city of "TJ" with the guys.

I wasn't on a single chemical substance after a decade of savage drug ABUSE.

It was a hoot. There was no crying family circled around me in a hotel meeting room, no rehab, no scrubbing toilets with toothbrushes, no maintenance meds, no cravings, no *disease.* I was just...done. It was like a science fiction movie, but, my friend, it wasn't; it was all real. I never tapered a milligram. In fact, I went on quite the bon voyage bender, the week prior. There were many things I didn't get around to doing while in Mexico: I didn't get to bribe a cop after doing cookies in front of him in the rental car, or go to "La Coahuila en Tijuana" with Carlo. Carlo really wanted to take me to La Coahuila. It was a street containing stores that "sold any drug you wanted."

Carlo claimed people stood in lines stretching "all the way around the corner." He called it the *McDonald's en Tijuana*. He seemed hell-bent on showing it to me, but it never happened. The truth is: I'd already seen and heard all I ever cared to know about drugs. I wouldn't have minded doing a little fishing, however, but the time just slipped away.

(Okay, so, I wasn't completely out of Edgar Poe's *woods* yet; after all, I still had to penetrate the American border. And, we all know how discriminating we are. So, get excited, because, here we go....)

On the day of my departure, I said goodbye to all of my new friends, and though I'd forged a friendship with everyone there, the truth is, I couldn't wait to get home. When it came to John, he said, "I won't be driving you back across the border, guy."

Instantly, it dawned on me why not. "There is no trouble *getting into Mexico without a passport*," is what John had said on the phone. Just then, I realized that...*getting into the US without a passport* was going to be a whole different challenge.

"Timmy, meet twin sisters, Nina, and Pinta. They are nurses here in Tijuana. They were already going to the border this morning, so we made arrangements for the sisters to drop you off at the airport," John said.

I couldn't be mad at John because I should have known better.

The two girls and I headed back north toward the Mexican-American border. That marked the first time I would ever get to see that stretch of the trip with clear eyes and I was looking forward to it. There were so many bizarre and fascinating things to see in that country.

John told us that some website had indicated it to be an opportune time for crossing the border. Therefore, the miles of lines that extended south from the checkpoint were spectacular and unexpected. Never have I seen so many window washers, street performers, and vendors.

"Holy blankets and ponchos."

Nina explained to me, "Tim, Tijuana is the busiest border in the entire world. See all those people living in the canal there? They are nearly all deportees from the US. Almost one hundred percent of those people are hooked on heroin, meth, or both. We have a cousin who is a volunteer social worker, and she passes out condoms and clean syringes down there. You wouldn't believe the stories.

"Many of the people were just as American as you with children, families, houses, and cars; many even had businesses there. We call them the 'plastic people.' One of my cousin's favorite people is a guy who lives in a burrow in the ground like an animal."

"He had a paid-off house and a mechanics shop up in the San Diego area. After 9/11 had occurred, the US tightened up the border and cracked down on immigration; he could no longer even register his car anymore.

"The guy had been living in San Diego for 18 years and had several grown children who were all born US citizens. One day he was picked-up by the police for having bad tags, and was deported; he's been living here in the Tijuana Canal ever since.

"He told my cousin that he had never been able to get a tax return in the US. The IRS held over one-hundred-thousand dollars in tax withholdings alone and if he had a fraction of that money he could afford to take a first-class private helicopter back across *El Bordo*. It's so sad," Nina finished.

Before Nina had finished her story, I was already crumpling up twenty-dollar-bills and discretely throwing them at the people who I had thought needed them most. I must have tossed one to every amputee and believe me; there were many of them. One of the nurse sisters noticed that I was throwing money out the window.

"Oh, my God, don't make that too obvious, or we'll all three be mobbed to death." I didn't care. I fired one at her and another at her sister, and they both hushed. The way each of those beautiful peoples' eyes lit up when they unfolded those bank notes, made my entire life worth living. While throwing twenties out the window, I moved from window-to-window in the backseat, until finally: A small mob began to form. The mob chased the car down the road as we advanced toward *El Bordo*. You would have thought I had dumped a ton of shelled sunflower seeds in the middle of Central Park.

"I told you so," Pinta said.

A motorcycle cop chirped his siren a couple of times and flashed his lights. The crowd disappeared into the adjacent canal in mere seconds through a hole in the fence. We pulled over. The cop spoke no English, so he spoke with the girls first. When the officer finished up with the girls; he turned to look at me. Without thinking, I threw one of the crumpled-up bills at the cop. The cop caught my rebound, after bouncing off his right mirrored sunglass-lens. The startled cop flinched, and just stared at me for a bit. Both girls gasped as they leaned back in their seats. The officer unfolded the crumpled twenty and examined it in the sunlight.

Upon confirming the bill's authenticity, he flicked the note with his finger, neatly folding the note, and tucking it into his shirt pocket. With a gloved finger, he tipped the thin, dark sun-brim on his helmet and walked back to his bike.

The driver rolled up her window, and the two girls shared the loudest laugh I had ever heard. (Well, now I can check bribing a cop off of my list.) We all laughed. The officer now trailed behind us and I continued to throw the wadded-up money to the chosen people. When someone wouldn't leave our car, or too many people had again gathered, the siren would again chirp, and they would quickly dissipate.

Soon, I was only holding ten, or so, twenty-dollar-bills, so I rolled up the back windows. We were within several cars of the border-patrol officer booth, plus our police escort had taken a turn, leaving us on our own. My stomach did a little somersault as I anticipated the inevitable interaction with the officer ahead.

The lines purified into a single-file and with only three more cars in front of us, the two sisters dropped one more bomb-shell upon me. The driver began to speak, "Before we get up to the officer, there are a few things that you need to know:

"First—you will mention nothing about the treatment you received there.

"Second—you will never reveal the location of the clinic.

"And finally, we're going to pretend not to speak English, and, you are not to acknowledge that you know we do speak English.

"Other than that—fair game—I don't give a shit what you say."

"Gee, thanks for giving me plenty of advanced notice to fabricate the story."

"Here, hand me your driver's license and passport," the driver requested as she aimlessly wafted her empty hand in front of my face. (I was sitting directly behind her.)

"Um, I don't have a passport."

"What do you mean, you don't have a pinche-passport?" the sisters asked in stereo.

"Nope… No passport," I confirmed.

"Fucking John!" the girls exclaimed.

The car in front of us motored off, and we advanced toward the booth. The officer wore a navy blue uniform and was sporting a tight blonde crew-cut. He looked to be in his mid-twenties.

"Good morning ma'am," the officer said with a thick southern draw. (YAHTZEE I knew I had a chance since I also spoke country boy.) He went through his whole spiel about firearms, drugs, fruit, and undocumented migrants; the agent then requested all of our documentation. The girls had some sort of quick-pass, but I seemed to be the person of interest there.

"Sir, can I see your passport please?" he asked, as he thumbed through the rest of the provided documentation.

"Sir, I am so sorry, but I didn't know that I'd be needing one of those to get into the country. The last time I came through here, I didn't need one."

"When was that?"

"Uh, eight or so years ago, I think," I ignorantly noted.

"Well, that law changed in January 2007—but you should have known that if you live in Arizona. Do you speak any Spanish?" the officer asked.

"No, not very much, sir," I said.

"Well, how is it, that these two ladies speak Spanish, and you don't, huh? What the hell is going on here? You're not being truthful with me," the officer said.

"Well, sir, I am going to be completely honest with you, now. I met these two young ladies online, okay? There, I admit it. I was on a creepy website through which all of our dialogue translated. It is one of those deals where you meet 'International Ladies of Interest' or some shit like that – I am so embarrassed? I never do this sort of thing officer. Obviously, we didn't need to speak much at all, you know?

"When we did need to communicate, we just texted each other on the ILI phone application—I pointed to my iPhone. Look, I am sorry…. But, surely there's some way we can clear this all up, right? Wait, I have a copy of my birth certificate in my bag in the back! Do you mind if I go back and grab it? It's not very good, though."

Upon hearing an "affirmative," I produced the document from the trunk and got back into the back-seat, alone.

"What is this?" the officer asked as he laughed hysterically.

"It is my birth certificate."

"This is no good, dude, but I'm gonna let you go through anyway. Never, ever, EVER make this mistake again, because there is a zero tolerance policy for entering the US now."

(The sea of people in the canal was proof of that.)

Page 253

"Just get out of here and don't tell anyone that I did this," he had nearly finished... *"Geez"*—the officer finally remarked.

The driver wasted no time evacuating that situation within the first syllable of a "go-ahead."

"That was dirty as hell but good," the driver said.

"You deserved that," I remarked as we all shared one last laugh.

We were back in the US again, but there was still tons of traffic, and I could tell that the twins didn't want to go to the airport. I told the girls to drop me off there on the road, and I would find my own ride; I could see the yellow of taxis peppered throughout the jam of cars.

"Oh no! Are you sure?" they asked.

The twins felt awful for letting on that they were annoyed. It was apparent that they were just frustrated with John. Everyone usually was; he was a free-spirit.

"Nah, go on without me, I got this."

Jumping out immediately, I double tapped the side of the car. My sense of smell was back, and the guys in TJ were exaggerating. The two countries smelled the same; it didn't smell different there. Not worse than what I'd smelled in New York or San Francisco, for example. Both are great cities: You just catch manhole whiffs and stuff, you know? The trunk popped up, and both sisters flung their entire upper bodies out of their respective windows.

The sisters waved and blew kisses, theatrically, to mock what I'd just said about them at the border. They accelerated in a juxtaposed direction while psychotically honking. I think they were just really happy since they no longer had to drive me to the San Diego airport.

A giant beam of what Mom used to call, *'Sunshine,'* stretched across my face while an enormous American flag waved in the chilly coastal wind. I enjoyed several miles of freedom before hailing a cab.

The End

...It *was* the end of my 'disease' of addiction. But I couldn't get that, *'riddle'* thing out of my head. *You know*....The riddle I *must* have solved in order to pass the two witches (in the camper) *who were in my visions*...for that you will have to read, *Sacred Scroll of Seven Seals,* by *'Judah.'* (An amazon.com #1 *Bestseller!*)

In Remembrance

Let us all take a moment to recognize my beautiful brother, *Joseph.* Who was a Godly creature, a loving Father, a wonderful human being, and a drug war hero, *and casualty.*

JOSEPH ALLEN ZIGLER
1973 – 2005